GRE

填空教程

○ 本书编写组　编

中国环境科学出版社
·北京·

教材说明

本GRE系列由《GRE类比·反义词教程》、《GRE填空教程》、《GRE数学教程》、《GRE阅读理解教程》、《GRE写作教程》和《最新GRE笔试模考练习》构成，由全国数十名著名GRE教学和研究专家历经数年集体编撰而成。

由于近年来GRE考试发生了一些变化，例如：作文改为机考了，语文、数学部分改在作文之后考了、词汇题也出现了不少新词，解题速度要求更高了等等。为了帮助广大同学适应上述变化，因此本系列涵盖了近十年的考试精华，尤其是涵盖了2002–2003年的最新考试趋势，真实地剖析和反映了ETS的出题思想及最新动态。

总之，本系列教材的实效性和实战性极强。广大同学只要使用本系列进行艰苦卓绝的训练，就一定能获得较理想的成绩。

2004年12月

目　录

Ex. 65-76
北美82-83

Directions: Each sentence below has one or two blanks, each blank indicating that something has been omitted. Beneath the sentence are five lettered words or set of words. Choose the word or set of words for each blank that best fits the meaning of the sentence as a whole.

Exercise 1

1. There are no solitary, free-living creatures; every form of life is______other forms.
   (A) segregated from
   (B) parallel to
   (C) dependent on
   (D) overshadowed by
   (E) mimicked by

2. As for the alleged value of expert opinion, one need only_______government records to see______ evidence of the failure of such opinions in many fields.
   (A) inspect...questionable
   (B) retain...circumstantial
   (C) distribute...possible
   (D) consult...strong
   (E) evaluate...problematic

3. Noting that few employees showed any______for complying with the corporation's new safety regulations, Peterson was forced to conclude that acceptance of the regulations would be_______, at best.
   (A) aptitude...unavoidable
   (B) regard...indeterminate
   (C) respect...negotiable
   (D) patience...imminent
   (E) enthusiasm...grudging

4. Yellow fever, the disease that killed 4,000 Philadelphians in 1793, and so______Memphis, Tennessee, that the city lost its charter, has reappeared after nearly two decades in_______in the Western Hemisphere.
   (A) terrorized...contention
   (B) ravaged...secret
   (C) disabled...quarantine

(D) corrupted...quiescence

(E) decimated...abeyance

5. Nature's energy efficiency often______human technology: despite the intensity of the light fireflies produce, the amount of heat is negligible; only recently have humans developed chemical light-producing systems whose efficiency______ the firefly's system.

(A) engenders...manipulates

(B) reflects...simulates

(C) outstrips...rivals

(D) inhibits...matches

(E) determines...reproduces

注意此题前后两个半句是反义关系！

6. Hampshire's assertions, far from showing that we can______the ancient puzzles about objectivity, reveal the issue to be even more______than we had thought.

(A) adapt...pressing

(B) dismiss...relevant 十分重大的；相关的

(C) rediscover...unconventional

(D) admire...elusive

(E) appreciate...interesting

7. Though extremely______about his own plans, the man allowed his associates no such privacy and was constantly______information about what they intended to do next.

(A) idiosyncratic...altering

(B) guarded...eschewing

(C) candid...uncovering

(D) reticent...soliciting

(E) fastidious...ruining

eschew 回避

reticent 有保留的

solicit 恳求、讨求

笔记区

Exercise 2

1. Heavily perfumed white flowers, such as gardenias, were favorites with collectors in the eighteenth century, when______was valued much more highly than it is today.

(A) scent

(B) beauty

(C) elegance

(D) color

(E) variety

2. At first, I found her gravity rather intimidating; but, as I saw more of her, I found that______was very near the surface.

(A) seriousness

(B) confidence

(C) laughter

(D) poise

(E) determination

3. The sheer bulk of data from the mass media seems to overpower us and drive us to______accounts for an easily and readily digestible portion of news.

(A) insular

(B) investigative

(C) synoptic

(D) subjective

(E) sensational

4. During the opera's most famous aria the tempo chosen by the orchestra's conductor seemed ______, without necessary relation to what had gone before.

(A) tedious

(B) melodious

(C) capricious

笔 记 区

(D) compelling
(E) cautious

5. Ironically, the party leaders encountered no greater ______their efforts to build a progressive party than the______of the progressives already elected to the legislature.
(A) support for...advocacy
(B) threat to...promise
(C) benefit from...success
(D) obstacle to...resistance
(E) praise for...reputation

6. No longer______by the belief that the world around us was expressly designed for humanity, many people try to find intellectual______for that lost certainty in astrology and in mysticism.
(A) satisfied...reasons
(B) sustained...substitutes
(C) reassured...justifications
(D) hampered...equivalents
(E) restricted...parallels

7. Just as astrology was for centuries______faith, countering the strength of established churches, so today believing in astrology is an act of______ the professional sciences.
(A) an individual...rebellion by
(B) an accepted...antagonism toward
(C) an underground...defiance against
(D) a heretical...support for
(E) an unknown...concern about

Exercise 3

1. Despite the fact that the two council members belonged to different political parties, they______ the issue of how to finance the town debt.
   (A) complicated
   (B) avoided
   (C) attested to
   (D) reported on
   (E) agreed on

2. Many of the earliest colonial houses that are still standing have been so modified and enlarged that the_______design is no longer______.
   (A) pertinent...relevant
   (B) intended...necessary
   (C) embellished...attractive
   (D) appropriate...applicable
   (E) initial...discernible

*3. Noting the murder victim's flaccid musculature and pearlike figure, she deduced that the unfortunate fellow had earned his living in some______occupation.
   (A) treacherous
   (B) prestigious
   (C) ill-paying
   (D) illegitimate
   (E) sedentary

4. Social tensions among adult factions can be______by politics, but adolescents and children have no such______for resolving their conflict with the exclusive world of adults.
   (A) intensified...attitude
   (B) complicated...relief
   (C) frustrated...justification

(D) adjusted...mechanism

(E) revealed...opportunity

5. Demonstrating a mastery of innuendo, he issued several______insults in the course of the evening's conversation. 含沙射影

(A) blunt

(B) veiled

(C) fallacious

(D) boisterous

(E) embellished

6. Because outlaws were denied______under medieval law, anyone could raise a hand against them with legal______.

(A) propriety...authority

(B) protection...impunity

(C) collusion...consent

(D) rights...collaboration

(E) provisions...validity

7. Parts of seventeenth-century Chinese pleasure gardens were not necessarily intended to look_____; they were designed expressly to evoke the agreeable melancholy resulting from a sense of the ______of natural beauty and human glory.

(A) beautiful...immutability

(B) cheerful...transitoriness

(C) colorful...abstractness

(D) luxuriant...simplicity

(E) conventional...wildness

EBDEBED
D E

Exercise 4

1. Since it is now______to build the complex central processing unit of a computer on a single silicon chip using photolithography and chemical etching, it seems plausible that other miniature structures might be fabricated in______ways.
   (A) unprecedented...undiscovered
   (B) difficult...related
   (C) permitted...unique
   (D) mandatory...congruent
   (E) routine...similar

2. The sale of Alaska was not so much an American coup as a matter of______for an imperial Russia that was short of cash and unable to______its own continental coastline.
   (A) negligence...fortify
   (B) custom...maintain
   (C) convenience...stabalize
   (D) expediency...defend
   (E) exigency...reinforce

3. Despite the______of many of their colleagues, some scholars have begun to emphasize "pop culture" as a key for______the myths, hopes, and fears of contemporary society.
   (A) antipathy...entangling
   (B) discernment...evaluating
   (C) pedantry...reinstating
   (D) skepticism...deciphering
   (E) enthusiasm...symbolizing

4. Edith Wharton sought in her memoir to present herself as having achieved a harmonious wholeness by having______the conflicting elements of her life.
   A) affirmed

笔 记 区

B) highlighted
C) identified
D) confined
E) reconciled

5. Rumors, embroidered with detail, live on for years, neither denied nor confirmed, until they become accepted as fact even among people not known for their______.
(A) insight
(B) obstinacy
(C) introspection
(D) tolerance
(E) credulity

6. Broadway audiences have become inured to______ and so______to be pleased as to make their ready ovations meaningless as an indicator of the quality of the production before them.
(A) sentimentality...reluctant
(B) condescension...disinclined
(C) histrionics...unlikely
(D) cleverness...eager
(E) mediocrity...desperate

7. Although he attempted repeatedly to______her of her conviction of his insincerity, he was not successful; she remained______in her judgment.
(A) remind...forceful
(B) convince...unfeigned
(C) exorcise...indulgent
(D) disabuse...adamant
(E) free...unsure

笔 记 区

Exercise 5

1. Psychology has slowly evolved into an______scientific discipline that now functions autonomously with the same privileges and responsibilities as other sciences.
   (A) independent
   (B) unusual
   (C) outmoded
   (D) uncontrolled
   (E) inactive

2. Just as such apparently basic things as rocks, clouds, and clams are, in fact, intricately structured entities, so the self, too, is not an "elementary particle," but is ______construction.
   (A) a complicated
   (B) a convoluted
   (C) a distorted
   (D) an amorphous
   (E) an illusory

3. The sociologist responded to the charge that her new theory was______by pointing out that it did not in fact contradict accepted sociological principles.
   (A) banal
   (B) heretical
   (C) unproven
   (D) complex
   (E) superficial

4. Since she believed him to be both candid and trustworthy, she refused to consider the possibility that his statement had been______.
   (A) irrelevant
   (B) facetious
   (C) mistaken

(D) critical
(E) insincere

5. The struggle of the generations is one of the obvious constants of human affairs; therefore, it may be presumptuous to suggest that the rivalry between young and old in Western society during the current decade is ______critical.
(A) perennially
(B) disturbingly
(C) uniquely
(D) archetypally 典型地
(E) captiously

6. It is ironic that a critic of such overwhelming vanity now suffers from a measure of the oblivion to which he was forever______others, in the end, all his______has only worked against him
(A) dedicating...self-procession
(B) leading...self-righteousness
(C) consigning...self-adulation
(D) relegating...self-sacrifice
(E) condemning...self-analysis

7. Melodramas, which presented stark oppositions between innocence and criminality, virtue and corruption, good and evil, were popular precisely because they offered the audience a world ______of______.
(A) bereft...theatricality
(B) composed...adversity
(C) full...circumstantiality
(D) deprived...polarity
(E) devoid...neutrality

Exercise 6

1. The spellings of many old English words have been______in the living language, although their pronunciations have changed.
   (A) preserved
   (B) shortened
   (C) preempted
   (D) revised
   (E) improved

2. Given the evidence of Egyptian and Babylonian ______later Greek civilization, it would be incorrect to view the work of Greek scientists as an entirely independent creation.
   (A) disdain for
   (B) imitation of
   (C) ambivalence about
   (D) deference to
   (E) influence on

3. Ecology, like economics, concerns itself with the movement of valuable______through a complex network of producers and consumers.
   (A) commodities
   (B) dividends
   (C) communications
   (D) nutrients
   (E) artifacts

4. The old man could not have been accused of______ his affection; his conduct toward the child betrayed his______her.
   (A) lavishing...fondness for
   (B) sparing...tolerance of
   (C) rationing...antipathy for

笔 记 区

(D) stinting...adoration of
(E) promising...dislike of

5. The new biological psychiatry does not deny the contributing role of psychological factors in mental illnesses, but posits that these factors may act as a catalyst on existing physiological conditions and ______such illnesses.
(A) disguise
(B) impede
(C) constrain
(D) precipitate
(E) consummate

6. Some scientists argue that carbon compounds play such a central role in life on Earth because of the possibility of______resulting from the carbon atom's ability to form an unending series of different molecules.
(A) deviation
(B) stability
(C) reproduction
(D) variety
(E) invigoration

7. That his intransigence in making decisions______no open disagreement from any quarter was well known; thus, clever subordinates learned the art of ______their opinions in casual remarks.
(A) elicited...quashing
(B) engendered...recasting
(C) brooked...intimating
(D) embodied...instigating
(E) forbore...emending

笔 记 区

Exercise 7

1. Dreams are______in and of themselves, but, when combined with other data, they can tell us much about the dreamer.
(A) uninformative
(B) startling
(C) harmless
(D) unregulated
(E) uncontrollable

2. In most Native American cultures, an article used in prayer or ritual is made with extraordinary attention to and richness of detail: it is decorated more______than a similar article intended for______use.
(A) delicately...vocational
(B) colorfully...festive
(C) creatively...religious
(D) subtly...commercial
(E) lavishly...everyday

3. The newborn human infant is not a passive figure, nor an active one, but what might be called an actively______one, eagerly attentive as it is to sights and sounds.
(A) adaptive
(B) selective
(C) inquisitive
(D) receptive
(E) intuitive

4. Before about 1960, virtually all accounts of evolution assumed most adaptation to be a product of selection at the level of populations; recent studies of evolution, however, have found no______this______view of selection.
(A) departures from....controversial
(B) basis for...pervasive

笔 记 区

(C) bias toward...unchallenged

(D) precursors of...innovative

(E) criticisms of...renowned

5. In the machinelike world of classical physics, the human intellect appears______, since the mechanical nature of classical physics does not ______creative reasoning, the very ability that had made the formulation of classical principles possible.

(A) anomalous...allow for

(B) abstract...speak to

(C) anachronistic...deny

(D) enduring...value

(E) contradictory...exclude

6. Although Johnson______great enthusiasm for his employees' project, in reality his interest in the project was so______as to be almost non-existent.

(A) generated...redundant

(B) displayed...preemptive

(C) expected...indiscriminate

(D) feigned...perfunctory

(E) demanded...dispassionate

7. Whereas the art critic Vasari saw the painting entitled the Mona Lisa as an original and wonderful______feat, the reproduction of a natural object, the aesthetes saw it as______that required deciphering.

(A) collaborative...an aberration

(B) historical...a symbol

(C) technical...a hieroglyph

(D) mechanical...an imitation

(E) visual...an illusion

笔 记 区

Exercise 8

1. Despite the apparently bewildering complexity of this procedure, the underlying______is quite______.
   (A) simplicity...calculated
   (B) principle...elementary
   (C) confusion...imaginary
   (D) purpose...effective
   (E) theory...modern

2. In spite of the______nature of Scotland's terrain,its main roads are surprisingly free from severe______.
   (A) rocky...weather
   (B) mountainous...grades
   (C) uncharted...flooding
   (D) unpredictable...damage
   (E) landlocked...slipperiness

3. While the delegate clearly sought to______the optimism that has emerged recently, she stopped short of suggesting that the conference was near collapse and might produce nothing of significance.
   (A) substantiate
   (B) dampen
   (C) encourage
   (D) elucidate
   (E) rekindle

4. The reduction of noise has been______in terms of______its sources, but the alternative of canceling noise out by adding sound with the opposite wave pattern may be more useful in practice.
   (A) justified...diffusing
   (B) accomplished...tracking

笔 记 区

(C) conceived...concealing

(D) explained...isolating

(E) approached...eliminating

5. While not completely nonplussed by the unusually caustic responses from members of the audience, the speaker was nonetheless visibly______by their lively criticism.

(A) humiliated

(B) discomfited

(C) deluded

(D) disgraced

(E) tantalized

6. During the 1960's assessments of the family shifted remarkably, from general endorsement of it as a worthwhile, stable institution to wide spread______it as an oppressive and bankrupt one whose______was both imminent and welcome.

(A) flight from...restitution

(B) fascination with...corruption

(C) rejection of...vogue

(D) censure of...dissolution

(E) relinquishment of...ascent

7*. Nineteenth-century scholars, by examining earlier geometric Greek art, found that classical Greek art was not a magical______or a brilliant______ blending Egyptian and Assyrian art, but was independently evolved by Greeks in Greece.

(A) stratagem...appropriation

(B) exemplar...synthesis

(C) conversion...annexation

(D) paradigm...construct

(E) apparition...amalgam

Exercise 9

1. As late as 1891 a speaker assured his audience that since profitable farming was the result of natural ability rather than______, an education in agriculture was______.

(A) instruction...vital

(B) effort...difficult

(C) learning...useless

(D) science...intellectual

(E) luck...senseless

2. A perennial goal in zoology is to infer function from______, relating the______of an organism to its physical form and cellular organization.

(A) age...ancestry

(B) classification...appearance

(C) size...movement

(D) structure...behavior

(E) location...habitat

3. Considering how long she had yearned to see Italy, her first reaction was curiously______.

(A) meditative

(B) tepid

(C) categorical

(D) unoriginal

(E) insightful

4. In Germany her startling powers as a novelist are widely______, but she is almost unknown in the English-speaking world because of the difficulties of ______her eccentric prose.

(A) ignored...editing

(B) admired...translating

(C) espoused...revealing

(D) obscured...comprehending

(E) dispersed...transcribing

5. In many science fiction films, the opposition of good and evil is portrayed as a______between technology, which is______, and the errant will of a depraved intellectual.

(A) fusion...useful

(B) struggle...dehumanizing

(C) parallel...unfettered

(D) conflict...beneficent

(E) similarity...malevolent

6. Comparatively few rock musicians are willing to laugh at themselves, although a hint of______can boost sales of video clips very nicely.

(A) self-deprecation

(B) congeniality

(C) cynicism

(D) embarrassment

(E) self-doubt

7. Within the next decade, sophisticated telescopes now orbiting the Earth will determine whether the continents really are moving, ______the incipient ______among geologists about the validity of the theory of continental drift.

(A) obviating...consensus

(B) forestalling...rift

(C) escalating...debates

(D) engendering...speculation

(E) resolving...rumors

Exercise 10

1. The commissions criticized the legislature for making college attendance dependent on the ability to pay, charging that, as a result, hundreds of qualified young people would be______further education.
   (A) entitled to
   (B) striving for
   (C) deprived of
   (D) uninterested in
   (E) participating in

2. In order to______her theory that the reactions are ______, the scientist conducted many experiments, all of which showed that the heat of the first reaction is more than twice that of the second.
   (A) support...different
   (B) comprehend...constant
   (C) evaluate...concentrated
   (D) capture...valuable
   (E) demonstrate...problematic

3. For centuries animals have been used as______ for people in experiments to assess the effects of therapeutic and other agents that might later be used in humans.
   (A) benefactors
   (B) companions
   (C) examples
   (D) precedents
   (E) surrogates

4. Having fully embraced the belief that government by persuasion is preferable to government by______, the leaders of the movement have recently______most of their previous statements supporting totalitarianism.
   (A) intimidation...issued

(B) participation...moderated

(C) proclamation...codified

(D) demonstration...deliberated

(E) coercion...repudiated

5. This final essay, its prevailing kindliness______by occasional flashes of savage irony, bespeaks the______character of the author.

(A) illuminated...imperturbable

(B) marred...dichotomous

(C) untainted...vindictive

(D) exemplified...chivalrous

(E) diluted...ruthless

6. Far from viewing Jefferson as a skeptical but enlightened intellectual, historians of the 1960's portrayed him as______thinker, eager to fill the young with his political orthodoxy while censoring ideas he did not like.

(A) an adventurous

(B) a doctrinaire

(C) an eclectic

(D) a judicious

(E) a cynical

7. Rather than enhancing a country's security, the successful development of nuclear weapons could serve at first to increase that country's __________.

(A) boldness

(B) influence

(C) responsibility

(D) moderation

(E) vulnerability

Exercise 11

1. After a slow sales start early in the year, mobile homes have been gaining favor as______to increasingly expensive conventional housing.
   (A) reaction
   (B) an addition
   (C) an introduction
   (D) an alternative
   (E) a challenge

2. A major goal of law, to deter potential criminals by punishing wrongdoers, is not served when the penalty is so seldom invoked that it______to be a _______threat.
   (A) tends...serious
   (B) appears...real
   (C) ceases...credible
   (D) fails...deceptive
   (E) seems...coercive

3. Even though in today's Soviet Union the______ the Muslim clergy have been accorded power and privileges, the Muslim laity and the rank-and-file clergy still have little______to practice their religion.
   (A) practitioners among...opportunity
   (B) dissidents within...obligation
   (C) adversaries of...inclination
   (D) leaders of...latitude
   (E) traditionalists among...incentive

4. The successful______of an archaeological site requires scientific knowledge as well as cultural______.
   (A) evolution...awareness
   (B) revelation...depth
   (C) reconstruction...sensitivity

笔 记 区

(D) analysis...aesthetics
(E) synthesis...understanding

5. New research on technology and public policy focuses on how seemingly ______design features, generally overlooked in most analyses of public works projects or industrial machinery, actually ___social choices of profound significance.
(A) insignificant...mask
(B) inexpensive...produce
(C) innovative...represent
(D) ingenious...permit
(E) inopportune...hasten

6. Individual freedom of thought should be______more absolutely than individual freedom of action, given that the latter, though also desirable, must be______the limits imposed by the rights and freedom of others.
(A) exercised...indifferent to
(B) assessed...measured by
(C) valued...superior to
(D) protected...subject to
(E) curtailed...conscious of

7. When theories formerly considered to be______ in their scientific objectivity are found instead to reflect a consistent observational and evaluative bias, then the presumed neutrality of science gives way to the recognition that categories of knowledge are human______.
(A) disinterested...constructions
(B) callous...errors
(C) verifiable...prejudices
(D) convincing...imperatives
(E) unassailable...fantasies

Exercise 12

1. Although the minuet appeared simple, its______ steps had to be studied very carefully before they could be gracefully______in public.
   (A) progressive...revealed
   (B) intricate...executed
   (C) rudimentary...allowed
   (D) minute...discussed
   (E) entertaining...stylized

2. Sponsors of the bill were______because there was no opposition to it within the legislature until after the measure had been signed into law.
   (A) unreliable
   (B) well-intentioned
   (C) persistent
   (D) relieved
   (E) detained

3. Dependence on foreign sources of heavy metals, though______, remains______for United States foreign policy.
   (A) deepening...a challenge
   (B) diminishing...a problem
   (C) excessive...a dilemma
   (D) debilitating...an embarrassment
   (E) unavoidable...a precedent

4. Although Mount Saint Helens has been more______during the last 4,500 years than any other volcano in the coterminous United States, its long dormancy before its recent eruption______its violent nature.
   (A) awe-inspiring...restrained
   (B) gaseous...confirmed
   (C) explosive...belied

笔 记 区

(D) familiar...moderated

(E) volatile...suggested

5. Liberty is not easy, but far better to be an ______fox, hungry and threatened on its hill, than a______ canary, safe and secure in its cage.

(A) unfriendly...fragile

(B) aging...young

(C) angry...content

(D) imperious...lethargic

(E) unfettered...well-fed

6. To test the______of borrowing from one field of study to enrich another, simply investigate the extent to which terms from the one may, without forcing, be______the other.

(A) risk...confused with

(B) universality...applied to

(C) decorum...illuminated by

(D) rate...superseded by

(E) efficacy...utilized by

7. Documenting science's______philosophy would be______, since it is almost axiomatic that many philosophers use scientific concepts as the foundations for their speculations.

(A) distrust of...elementary

(B) influence on...superfluous

(C) reliance on...inappropriate

(D) dependence on...difficult

(E) differences from...impossible

Exercise 13

1. Hydrogen is the ______element of the universe in that it provides the building blocks from which the other elements are produced.
   (A) steadiest
   (B) expendable
   (C) lightest
   (D) final
   (E) fundamental

2. The breathing spell provided by the______arms shipments should give all the combatants a chance to reevaluate their positions.
   (A) plethora of
   (B) moratorium on
   (C) reciprocation of
   (D) concentration on
   (E) development of

3. The wonder of De Quincey is that although opium dominated his life, it never______him; indeed, he turned its use to______when he published the story of its influence in the London Magazine.
   (A) overcame...altruism
   (B) intimidated...triumph
   (C) distressed...pleasure
   (D) conquered...gain
   (E) released...necessity

4. It has been argued that politics as______, whatever its transcendental claims, has always been the systematic organization of common hatreds.
   (A) a theory
   (B) an ideal
   (C) a practice

笔 记 区

(D) a contest
(E) an enigma

5. While she initially suffered the fate of many pioneers—the incomprehension of her colleagues—octogenarian Nobel laureate Barbara McClintock has lived to______the triumph of her once______scientific theories.
(A) descry...innovative
(B) regret...insignificant
(C) perpetuate...tentative
(D) enjoy...authoritative
(E) savor...heterodox

6. In failing to see that the justice's pronouncement merely______previous decisions rather than actually establishing a precedent, the novice law clerk______the scope of the justice's judgment.
(A) synthesized...limited
(B) overturned...misunderstood
(C) endorsed...nullified
(D) qualified...overemphasized
(E) recapitulated...defined

7. Early critics of Emily Dickinson's poetry mistook for simplemindedness the surface of artlessness that in fact she constructed with such______.
(A) astonsishment
(B) cunning
(C) allusion
(D) innocence
(E) vexation

Exercise 14

1. Her______should not be confused with miserliness; as long as I have known her, she has always been willing to assist those who are in need.
(A) intemperance
(B) intolerance
(C) apprehension
(D) diffidence
(E) frugality

2. Few of us take the pains to study our cherished convictions; indeed, we almost have a natural___ doing so.
(A) aptitude for
(B) repugnance to
(C) interest in
(D) ignorance of
(E) reaction after

3. Without the psychiatrist's promise of confidentiality, trust is______and the patient's communication limited; even though confidentiality can thus be seen to be precious in therapy, moral responsibility sometimes requires a willingness to______it.
(A) implicit...extend
(B) ambiguous...apply
(C) prevented...uphold
(D) assumed...examine
(E) impaired...sacrifice

4. Adam Smith's Wealth of Nations (1776) is still worth reading, more to appreciate the current_______of Smith's valid contributions to economics than to see those contributions as the ______of present-day economics.
(A) disregard...outgrowths
(B) reaffirmation...concerns

(C) relevance...precursors
(D) acceptance...byproducts
(E) importance...vestiges

5. While Parker is very outspoken on issues she cares about, she is not______; she concedes the______of opposing arguments when they expose weaknesses inherent in her own.
(A) fickle...validity
(B) arrogant...restraint
(C) fanatical...strength
(D) congenial...incompatibility
(E) unyielding...speciousness

6. Although the revelation that one of the contestants was a friend left the judge open to charges of lack of______, the judge remained adamant in her assertion that acquaintance did not necessarily imply______.
(A) prudence...tolerance
(B) detachment...foreknowledge
(C) exoneration...impropriety
(D) prejudice...preference
(E) disinterestedness...partiality

7. Exposure to sustained noise has been claimed to______blood pressure regulation in human beings and, particularly, to increase hypertension, even though some researchers have obtained inconclusive results that______the relationship.
(A) sharpen...conflate
(B) increase...diminish
(C) aggravate...buttress
(D) disrupt...neutralize
(E) impair...obscure

笔 记 区

Exercise 15

1. Although the feeding activities of whales and walruses give the seafloor of the Bering Shelf a devastated appearance, these activities seem to be actually______to the area, ______its productivity.
(A) destructive...counterbalancing
(B) rehabilitative...diminishing
(C) beneficial...enhancing
(D) detrimental...redirecting
(E) superfluous...encumbering

2. As long as nations cannot themselves accumulate enough physical power to dominate all others, they must depend on______.
(A) allies
(B) resources
(C) freedom
(D) education
(E) self-determination

3. The paradoxical aspect of the myths about Demeter, when we consider the predominant image of her as a tranquil and serene goddess, is her______search for her daughter.
(A) extended
(B) agitated
(C) comprehensive
(D) motiveless
(E) heartless

4. The proponents of recombinant DNA research have decided to______federal regulation of their work; they hope that by making this compromise they can forestall proposed state and local controls that might be even stiffer.
(A) protest

笔 记 区

(B) institute
(C) deny
(D) encourage
(E) disregard

5. At several points in his discussion, Graves, in effect, ______evidence when it does not support his argument, tailoring it to his needs.
(A) addresses
(B) creates
(C) alters
(D) suppresses
(E) substitutes

6. Our new tools of systems analysis, powerful though they may be, lead to______theories, especially, and predictably, in economics and political science, where productive approaches have long been highly______.
(A) pragmatic...speculative
(B) inelegant...efficacious
(C) explanatory...intuitional
(D) wrongheaded...convergent
(E) simplistic...elusive

7. The ______questions that consistently structure the study of history must be distinguished from merely______questions, which have their day and then pass into oblivion.
(A) recurrent...practical
(B) instinctive...factual
(C) ingrained...discriminating
(D) philosophical...random
(E) perennial...ephemeral

Exercise 16

1. Many artists believe that successful imitation, far from being symptomatic of a lack of______, is the first step in learning to be creative.
   (A) elegance
   (B) resolution
   (C) goodness
   (D) originality
   (E) sympathy

2. The sheer diversity of tropical plants represents a seemingly______source of raw materials, of which only a few have been utilized.
   (A) exploited
   (B) quantifiable
   (C) controversial
   (D) inexhaustible
   (E) remarkable

3. Having no sense of moral obligation, Shipler was as little subject to the______of conscience after he acted as he was motivated by its______before he acted.
   (A) rewards...chastisement
   (B) balm...eloquence
   (C) reproaches...promptings
   (D) ridicule...allure
   (E) qualms...atonement

4. Charlotte Salomon's biography is a reminder that the currents of private life, however diverted, dislodged, or twisted by ______public events, retain their hold on the______recording them.
   (A) transitory...culture
   (B) dramatic...majority
   (C) overpowering...individual

(D) conventional...audience
(E) relentless...institution

5. Longdale and Stern discovered that mitochondria and chloroplasts______a long, identifiable sequence of DNA; such a coincidence could be______only by the transfer of DNA between the two systems.
(A) manufacture...accomplished
(B) reveal...repeated
(C) exhibit...determined
(D) share...explained
(E) maintain...contradicted

6. Scholars' sense of the uniqueness of the central concept of "the state" at the time when political science became an academic field quite naturally led to striving for a correspondingly______mode of study.
(A) thorough
(B) distinctive
(C) dependable
(D) scientific
(E) dynamic

7. Any language is a conspiracy against experience in the sense that it is a collective attempt to______ experience by reducing it into discrete parcels.
(A) extrapolate
(B) transcribe
(C) complicate
(D) amplify
(E) manage

Exercise 17

1. It was a war the queen and her more prudent counselors wished to______if they could and were determined in any event to______as long as possible.
(A) provoke...delay
(B) denounce...deny
(C) instigate...conceal
(D) curtail...promote
(E) avoid...postpone

2. As the first streamlined car, the Airflow represented a______in automotive development, and although its sales were______, it had an immense influence on automobile design.
(A) revolution...tolerable
(B) breakthrough...significant
(C) regression...unimportant
(D) misjudgment...calculable
(E) milestone...disappointing

3. Walpole's art collection was huge and fascinating, and his novel *The Castle of Otranto* was never out of print; none of this mattered to the Victorians, who______him as, at best, ______.
(A) dismissed...insignificant
(B) judged...worthwhile
(C) revered...talented
(D) reviled...meager
(E) taunted...dangerous

4. Since the author frequently______other scholars, his objection to disputes is not only irrelevant but also______.
(A) supports...overbearing
(B) provokes...frightening

(C) quotes...curious
(D) ignores...peevish
(E) attacks...surprising

5. A war, even if fought for individual liberty and democratic rights, usually requires that these principles be______, for they are______the regimentation and discipline necessary for military efficiency.
(A) espoused...contrary to
(B) suppressed...fulfilled through
(C) suspended...incompatible with
(D) followed...disruptive of
(E) rejected...inherent in

6. In the design of medical experiments, the need for______assignment of treatments to patients must be______the difficulty of persuading patients to participate in an experiment in which their treatment is decided by chance.
(A) independent...amended by
(B) competent...emphasized by
(C) random...reconciled with
(D) swift...associated with
(E) mechanical...controlled by

7. Not all the indicators necessary to convey the effect of depth in a picture work simultaneously; the picture's illusion of______three-dimensional appearance must therefore result from the viewer's integration of various indicators perceived______.
(A) imitative...coincidentally
(B) uniform...successively
(C) temporary...comprehensively
(D) expressive...sympathetically
(E) schematic...passively

笔 记 区

Exercise 18

1. Animals that have tasted unpalatable plants tend to______them afterward on the basis of their most conspicuous features, such as their flowers.
(A) recognize
(B) hoard
(C) trample
(D) retrieve
(E) approach

2. There is some______the fact that the author of a book as sensitive and informed as *Indian Artisans* did not develop her interest in Native American art until adulthood, for she grew up in a region rich in American Indian culture.
(A) irony in
(B) satisfaction in
(C) doubt about
(D) concern about
(E) presumptuousness in

3. The notion that cultural and biological influences______determine cross-cultural diversity is discredited by the fact that, in countless aspects of human existence, it is cultural programming that overwhelmingly accounts for cross-population variance.
(A) jointly
(B) completely
(C) directly
(D) equally
(E) eventually

4. Even those who disagreed with Carmen's views rarely faulted her for expressing them, for the positions she took were as______as they were controversial.
(A) complicated

笔 记 区

(B) political
(C) subjective
(D) commonplace
(E) thoughtful

5. Number theory is rich in problems of an especially______sort: they are tantalizingly simple to state but______difficult to solve.
(A) cryptic...deceptively
(B) spurious...equally
(C) abstruse...ostensibly
(D) elegant...rarely
(E) vexing ...notoriously

6. It is strange how words shape our thoughts and trap us at the bottom of deeply______canyons of thinking, their imprisoning sides carved out by the ______of past usage.
(A) cleaved...eruptions
(B) rooted...flood
(C) incised...river
(D) ridged...ocean
(E) notched...mountains

7. Without seeming unworldly, William James appeared wholly removed from the______of society, the conventionality of academe.
(A) ethos
(B) idealism
(C) romance
(D) paradoxes
(E) commonplaces

Exercise 19

1. In the current research program, new varieties of apple trees are evaluated under different agricultural______for tree size, bloom density, fruit size, ______to various soils, and resistance to pests and disease.
   (A) circumstances...proximity
   (B) regulations...conformity
   (C) conditions...adaptability
   (D) auspices...susceptibility
   (E) configurations...propensity

2. Cryogenic energy storage has the advantage of being suitable in any______, regardless of geography or geology, factors that may______ both underground gas storage and pumped hydroelectric storage.
   (A) location...limit
   (B) climate...deter
   (C) site...forebode 预言,预兆
   (D) proportion...typify
   (E) surface...hamper

3. No one is______about Stephens; he inspires either uncritical adulation or profound______in those who work for him.
   (A) neutral...antipathy
   (B) infuriated...aversion
   (C) worried...anxiety
   (D) enthusiastic...veneration 尊敬
   (E) apprehensive...consternation

4. Opponents of the expansion of the market economy, although in______, continued to constitute______political force throughout the century.
   (A) error...an inconsequential
   (B) retreat...a powerful

笔 记 区

(C) disarray...a disciplined
(D) jeopardy...an ineffective
(E) command...a viable

5. The powers and satisfactions of primeval people, though few and meager, were_______ their few and simple desires.
(A) simultaneous with
(B) commensurate with
(C) substantiated by
(D) circumscribed by
(E) ruined by

6. Among the many______of the project, expense cannot be numbered; the goals of the project's promoters can be achieved with impressive______.
(A) highlights...efficiency
(B) features...savings
(C) disadvantages...innovation
(D) claims...speed
(E) defects...economy

7. The self-important cant of musicologists on record jackets often suggests that true appreciation of the music is an______process closed to the uninitiated listener, however enthusiastic.
(A) unreliable
(B) arcane
(C) arrogant
(D) elementary
(E) intuitive

Exercise 20

1. Though it would be______to expect Barnard to have worked out all of the limitations of his experiment, he must be______for his neglect of quantitative analysis.
(A) unjust...pardoned
(B) impudent...dismissed
(C) unrealistic...criticized
(D) pointless...examined
(E) inexcusable...recognized

2. The Muses are______deities: they avenge themselves without mercy on those who weary of their charms.
(A) rueful
(B) ingenuous
(C) solicitous
(D) vindictive
(E) dispassionate

3. We realized that John was still young and impressionable, but were nevertheless surprised at his______.
(A) naivete
(B) obstinateness
(C) decisiveness
(D) ingeniousness
(E) resolve

4. Although Johnson's and Smith's initial fascination with the fortunes of those jockeying for power in the law firm______after a few months, the two paid sufficient attention to determine who their lunch partners should be.
(A) revived
(B) emerged
(C) intensified

笔记区

(D) flagged

(E) persisted

5. As painted by Constable, the scene is not one of bucolic______; rather it shows a striking emotional and intellectual______.

(A) intensity...boredom

(B) complacence...detachment

(C) serenity...tension

(D) vitality...excitement

(E) nostalgia...placidity

6. Rhetoric often seems to______over reason in a heated debate, with both sides______in hyperbole.

(A) cloud...subsiding

(B) prevail...yielding

(C) triumph...engaging

(D) reverberate...clamoring

(E) trample...tangling

7. People should not be praised for their virtue if they lack the energy to be______; in such cases, goodness is merely the effect of______.

(A) depraved...hesitation

(B) cruel...effortlessness

(C) wicked...indolence

(D) unjust...boredom

(E) iniquitous...impiety

Exercise 21

1. Created to serve as perfectly as possible their workaday______, the wooden storage boxes made in America's Shaker communities are now______for their beauty.
(A) environment...accepted
(B) owners...employed
(C) function...valued
(D) reality...transformed
(E) image...seen

2. In a most impressive demonstration, Pavarotti sailed through Verdi's "*Celeste Aida*," normally a tenor's ______, with the casual enthusiasm of a folk singer performing one of his favorite______.
(A) pitfall...recitals
(B) glory...chorales
(C) nightmare...ballads
(D) delight...chanteys
(E) routine...composers

3. The cultivation of the emotion of natsukashii, interpretable as "pleasant sorrow," brings Japanese to Kyoto in the spring, not to______the cherry blossoms in full bloom but to______the fading, falling flowers.
(A) mourn...exclaim over
(B) honor...protect
(C) describe...rejoice over
(D) arrange...preserve
(E) savor...grieve over

4. The primary criterion for______a school is its recent performance: critics are______to extend credit for earlier victories.
(A) evaluating ...prone
(B) investigating ...hesitant

(C) judging ...reluctant

(D) improving ...eager

(E) administering ...persuaded

5. The significance of the Magna Carta lies not in its______provisions, but in its broader impact: it made the king subject to the law.

(A) revolutionary

(B) specific

(C) implicit

(D) controversial

(E) finite

6. Until the current warming trend exceeds the range of normal climatic fluctuations, there will be, among scientists, considerable______the possibility that increasing levels of atmospheric CO_2 can cause long-term warming effects.

(A) interest in

(B) uncertainty about

(C) enthusiasm for

(D) worry about

(E) experimentation on

7. Though science is often imagined as a_______ exploration of external reality, scientists are no different from anyone else: they are______human beings enmeshed in a web of personal and social circumstances.

(A) fervent...vulnerable

(B) neutral...rational

(C) painstaking...careless

(D) disinterested...passionate

(E) cautious...dynamic

Exercise 22

1. Although adolescent maturational and developmental states occur in an orderly sequence, their timing______with regard to onset and duration.
(A) lasts
(B) varies
(C) falters
(D) accelerates
(E) dwindles

2. Natural selection tends to eliminate genes that cause inherited diseases, acting most strongly against the most severe diseases; consequently, hereditary diseases that are______would be expected to be very______, but, surprisingly, they are not.
(A) lethal...rare
(B) untreated...dangerous
(C) unusual...refractory
(D) new...perplexing
(E) widespread...acute

3. It is his dubious distinction to have proved what nobody would think of denying, that Romero at the age of sixty-four writes with all the characteristics of______.
(A) maturity
(B) fiction
(C) inventiveness
(D) art
(E) brilliance

4. A common argument claims that in folk art, the artist's subordination of technical mastery to intense feeling______the direct communication of emotion to the viewer.
(A) facilitates
(B) averts
(C) neutralizes

笔 记 区

(D) implies

(E) represses

5. It is to the novelist's credit that all of the episodes in her novel are presented realistically, without any______or playful supernatural tricks.

(A) elucidation

(B) discrimination

(C) artlessness

(D) authenticity

(E) whimsy

6. Although his attempts to appear psychotic were so______as to be almost______, there is evidence that Ezra Pound was able to avoid standing trial for treason merely by faking symptoms of mental illness.

(A) spontaneous...amusing

(B) contrived...believable

(C) clumsy...ludicrous

(D) stylized...distressing

(E) sporadic...premeditated

7. The First World War began in a context of jargon and verbal delicacy and continued in a cloud of______as______as language and literature, skillfully used, could make it.

(A) circumlocution...literal

(B) cliche...lucid

(C) euphemism...impenetrable

(D) particularity...deliberate

(E) subjectivity...enthralling

Exercise 23

1. The discovery that, friction excluded, all bodies fall at the same rate is so simple to state and to grasp that there is a tendency to______its significance.
   (A) underrate
   (B) control
   (C) reassess
   (D) praise
   (E) eliminate

2. Although skeptics say financial problems will probably______our establishing a base on the Moon; supporters of the project remain______, saying that human curiosity should overcome such pragmatic constraints.
   (A) beset...disillusioned
   (B) hasten...hopeful
   (C) postpone...pessimistic
   (D) prevent...enthusiastic
   (E) allow...unconvinced

3. Despite assorted effusions to the contrary, there is no necessary link between scientific skill and humanism, and, quite possibly, there may be something of a______between them.
   (A) generality
   (B) fusion
   (C) congruity
   (D) dichotomy
   (E) reciprocity

4. Cynics believe that people who______compliments do so in order to be praised twice.
   (A) bask in
   (B) give out

笔 记 区

(C) despair of
(D) gloat over
(E) shrug off

5. Changes of fashion and public taste are often___and resistant to analysis, and yet they are among the most______gauges of the state of the public's collective consciousness.
(A) transparent...useful
(B) ephemeral...sensitive
(C) faddish...underutilized
(D) arbitrary...problematic
(E) permanent...reliable

6. During periods of social and cultural stability, many art academies are so firmly controlled by______that all real creative work must be done by the______.
(A) dogmatists...disenfranchised
(B) managers...reactionaries
(C) reformers...dissatisfied
(D) imposters...academicians
(E) specialists...elite

7. Usually the first to spot data that were inconsistent with other findings, in this particular experiment she let a number of______results slip by.
(A) inaccurate
(B) verifiable
(C) redundant
(D) salient
(E) anomalous

Exercise 24

1. Because no comprehensive______exist regarding personal reading practices, we do not know, for example, the greatest number of books read in an individual lifetime.
   (A) records
   (B) instincts
   (C) remedies
   (D) proposals
   (E) commercials

2. In television programming, a later viewing time often______a more______audience and, therefore, more challenging subjects and themes.
   (A) requires...critical
   (B) evinces...affluent
   (C) implies...mature
   (D) eliminates...realistic
   (E) invites...general

3. Unfortunately, his damaging attacks on the ramifications of the economic policy have been______by his wholehearted acceptance of that policy's underlying assumptions.
   (A) supplemented
   (B) undermined
   (C) wasted
   (D) diverted
   (E) redeemed

4. Speakers and listeners are often at odds: language that is easy for the receiver to understand is often difficult to______, and that which is easily formulated can be hard to______
   (A) produce...comprehend
   (B) transmit...defend

笔 记 区

(C) estimate...confirm
(D) suppress...ignore
(E) remember...forget

5. Philosophical problems arise when people ask questions that, though very______, have certain characteristics in common.
(A) relevant
(B) elementary
(C) abstract
(D) diverse
(E) controversial

6. In eighth-century Japan, people who______ wasteland were rewarded with official ranks as part of an effort to overcome the shortage of______fields.
(A) conserved...forested
(B) reclaimed...arable
(C) cultivated...domestic
(D) irrigated...accessible
(E) located...desirable

7. Famous among job seekers for its______, the company, quite apart from generous salaries, bestowed on its executives annual bonuses and such______as low-interest home mortgages and company cars.
(A) magnanimity...reparations
(B) inventiveness...benefits
(C) largesse...perquisites
(D) discernment...prerogatives
(E) altruism...credits

笔 记 区

Exercise 25

1. By divesting himself of all regalities, the former king______the consideration that customarily protects monarchs.
   (A) merited
   (B) forfeited
   (C) debased
   (D) concealed
   (E) extended

2. As serious as she is about the bullfight, she does not allow respect to______her sense of whimsy when painting it.
   (A) inspire
   (B) provoke
   (C) suppress
   (D) attack
   (E) satisfy

3. When people are happy, they tend to give______ interpretations of events they witness: the eye of the beholder is______by the emotions of the beholder.
   (A) charitable...colored
   (B) elaborate...disquieted
   (C) conscientious...deceived
   (D) vague...sharpened
   (E) coherent...confused

4. Observable as a tendency of our culture is a ________of ________psychoanalysis: we no longer feel that it can solve our emotional problems.
   (A) divergence...certainty about
   (B) confrontation...enigmas in
   (C) withdrawal...belief in
   (D) defense...weaknesses in

(E) failure...rigor in

5. The state is a network of exchanged benefits and beliefs, ______between rulers and citizens based on those laws and procedures that are______to the maintenance of community.

(A) a compromise...inimical

(B) an interdependence...subsidiary

(C) a counterpoint...incidental

(D) an equivalence...prerequisite

(E) a reciprocity...conducive

6. Regardless of what______theories of politics may propound, there is nothing that requires daily politics to be clear, thorough, and consistent — nothing, that is, that requires reality to conform to theory.

(A) vague

(B) assertive

(C) casual

(D) vicious

(E) tidy

7. Cezanne's delicate watercolor sketches often served as______of a subject, a way of gathering fuller knowledge before the artist's final engagement of the subject in an oil painting.

(A) an abstraction

(B) an enhancement

(C) a synthesis

(D) a reconnaissance 侦察、勘测

(E) a transcription 抄写，标音

Exercise 26

1. The natural balance between prey and predator has been increasingly______, most frequently by human intervention.
   (A) celebrated
   (B) predicted
   (C) observed
   (D) disturbed
   (E) questioned

2. The results of the experiments performed by Elizabeth Hazen and Rachel Brown were______not only because these results challenged old assumptions but also because they called the______ methodology into question.
   (A) provocative...prevailing
   (B) predictable...contemporary
   (C) inconclusive...traditional
   (D) intriguing...projected
   (E) specious...original

3. In scientific inquiry, it becomes a matter of duty to expose a ______hypothesis to every possible kind of______.
   (A) tentative...examination
   (B) debatable...approximation
   (C) well-established...rationalization
   (D) logical...elaboration
   (E) suspect...correlation

4. Freud derived psychoanalytic knowledge of childhood indirectly: he______childhood processes from adult______.
   (A) reconstructed...memory
   (B) condoned...experience
   (C) incorporated...behavior

(D) released...monotony
(E) inferred...anticipation

5. Current data suggest that, although______states between fear and aggression exist, fear and aggression are as distinct physiologically as they are psychologically.
(A) simultaneous
(B) serious
(C) exceptional
(D) partial
(E) transitional

6. Our times seem especially ______to bad ideas, probably because in throwing off the shackles of tradition, we have ended up being quite______untested theories and untried remedies.
(A) impervious...tolerant of
(B) hostile...dependent on
(C) hospitable...vulnerable to
(D) prone...wary of
(E) indifferent...devoid of

7. In recent decades the idea that Cezanne influenced Cubism has been caught in the______between art historians who credit Braque with its invention and those who______Picasso.
(A) crossfire...tout
(B) interplay...advocate
(C) paradox...prefer
(D) deliberation...attribute
(E) tussle...substitute

笔 记 区

CBCAADB C

Exercise 27

1. Clearly refuting sceptic, researchers have______not only that gravitational radiation exists but that it also does exactly what theory______it should do.
   (A) doubted...warranted
   (B) estimated...accepted
   (C) demonstrated...predicted
   (D) assumed...deduced
   (E) supposed...asserted

2. In our corporation there is a______between male and female______because 73 percent of the men and 34 percent of the women polled believe that our company provides equal compensation to men and women.
   (A) contrast...stereotypes
   (B) difference...perceptions
   (C) variation...salaries
   (D) resemblance...employees
   (E) similarity...aspirations

3. Scientists' pristine reputation as devotees of the disinterested pursuit of truth has been_____by recent evidence that some scientists have deliberately ______experimental results to further their own careers.
   (A) reinforced...published
   (B) validated...suppressed
   (C) exterminated...replicated
   (D) compromised...fabricated
   (E) resuscitated...challenged

4. Because medieval women's public participation in spiritual life was not welcomed by the male establishment, a compensating______religious writings, inoffensive to the members of the establishment because of its______, became important for many women.

笔 记 区

(A) involvement with...privacy
(B) attention to...popularity
(C) familiarity with...scarcity
(D) dissatisfaction with...profundity
(E) resistance to...domesticity

5. Queen Elizabeth I has quite correctly been called a ______of the arts, because many young artists received her patronage.
(A) connoisseur
(B) critic
(C) friend
(D) scourge 祸害
(E) judge

6. Although scientists claim that the seemingly______ language of their reports is more precise than the figurative language of fiction, the language of science, like all language, is inherently______.
(A) ornamental...subtle
(B) unidimensional...unintelligible
(C) symbolic...complex
(D) literal...allusive
(E) subjective...metaphorical

7. The English novelist William Thackeray considered the cult of the criminal so dangerous that he criticized Dickens' *Oliver Twist* for making the characters in the thieves' kitchen so______.
(A) threatening
(B) riveting
(C) conniving
(D) fearsome
(E) irritating

Exercise 28

1. There is perhaps some truth in that waggish old definition of a scholar—a siren that calls attention to a fog without doing anything to_______it.
(A) describe
(B) cause
(C) analyze
(D) dispel
(E) thicken

2. The hierarchy of medical occupations is in many ways a_______system; its strata remain_______and the practitioners in them have very little vertical mobility.
(A) health...skilled
(B) delivery...basic
(C) regimental...flexible
(D) training...inferior
(E) caste...intact

3. The prospects of discovering new aspects of the life of a painter as thoroughly studied as Vermeer are not, on the surface, _______
(A) encouraging
(B) daunting
(C) unpromising
(D) superficial
(E) challenging

4. In the seventeenth century, direct flouting of a generally accepted system of values was regarded as_______, even as a sign of madness.
(A) adventurous
(B) frivolous
(C) willful
(D) impermissible

笔 记 区

(E) irrational

5. Although nothing could be further from the truth, freight railroads have been______of______the nation's shift from oil to coal by charging exorbitant fees to transport coal.
(A) accused...impeding
(B) proud...accelerating
(C) guilty...delaying
(D) conscious...contributing to
(E) wary...interfering with

6. The poet W. H. Auden believed that the greatest poets of his age were almost necessarily irresponsible, that the possession of great gifts______the______to abuse them.
(A) negates...temptation
(B) controls...resolution
(C) engenders...propensity
(D) tempers...proclivity
(E) obviates...inclination

7. Johnson never______to ignore the standards of decent conduct mandated by company policy if______compliance with instructions from his superiors enabled him to do so, whatever the effects on his subordinates.
(A) deigned...tacit
(B) attempted...halfhearted
(C) intended...direct
(D) scrupled...literal
(E) wished...feigned

Exercise 29

1. Social scientists have established fairly clear-cut______that describe the appropriate behavior of children and adults, but there seems to be______ about what constitutes appropriate behavior for adolescents.
   (A) functions...rigidity
   (B) estimates...indirectness
   (C) norms...confusion
   (D) regulations...certainty
   (E) studies...misapprehension

2. Their mutual teasing seemed______, but in fact it ______a long-standing hostility.
   (A) aimless...produced
   (B) friendly...masked
   (C) playful...contravened
   (D) bitter...revealed
   (E) clever...averted

3. Her first concert appearance was disappointingly perfunctory and derivative, rather than the______performance in the______style we had anticipated.
   (A) talented...tenuous
   (B) inspired...innovative
   (C) artistic...mechanical
   (D) prosaic...classic
   (E) literal...enlightened

4. Industrialists seized economic power only after industry had______agriculture as the preeminent form of production; previously such power had ______land ownership.
   (A) sabotaged...threatened
   (B) overtaken...produced
   (C) toppled...culminated in

笔 记 区

(D) joined...relied on

(E) supplanted...resided in

5. Although______, almost self-effacing in his private life, he displays in his plays and essays a strong ______publicity and controversy.

(A) conventional...interest in

(B) monotonous...reliance on

(C) shy...aversion toward

(D) retiring...penchant for

(E) evasive...impatience with

6. Remelting old metal cans rather than making primary aluminum from bauxite ore shipped from overseas saves producers millions of dollars in______ and production costs.

(A) distribution

(B) salvage

(C) storage

(D) procurement

(E) research

7. To have true disciples, a thinker must not be too ______: any effective intellectual leader depends on the ability of other people to______thought processes that did not originate with them.

(A) popular...dismiss

(B) methodical...interpret

(C) idiosyncratic...reenact

(D) self-confident...revitalize

(E) pragmatic...discourage

笔 记 区

Exercise 30

1. Vaillant, who has been particularly interested in the means by which people attain mental health, seems to be looking for______answers: a way to close the book on at least a few questions about human nature.
(A) temporary
(B) confused
(C) definitive
(D) personal
(E) derivative

2. In an age without radio or recordings, an age______ by print, fiction gained its greatest ascendancy.
(A) decimated
(B) denigrated
(C) dominated
(D) emphasized
(E) resurrected

3. Laws do not ensure social order since laws can always be______, which makes them______unless the authorities have the will and the power to detect and punish wrongdoing.
(A) contested...provisional
(B) circumvented...antiquated
(C) repealed...vulnerable
(D) violated...ineffective
(E) modified...unstable

4. William James lacked the usual______death; writing to his dying father, he spoke without______about the old man's impending death.
(A) longing for...regret
(B) awe of...inhibition

笔 记 区

(C) curiosity about...rancor
(D) apprehension of...eloquence
(E) anticipation of...commiseration

5. A leading chemist believes that many scientists have difficulty with stereochemistry because much of the relevant nomenclature is______, in that it combines concepts that should be kept______.
(A) obscure...interrelated
(B) specialized...intact
(C) subtle...inviolate
(D) descriptive...separate
(E) imprecise...discrete

6. Paradoxically, Robinson's excessive denials of the worth of early works of science fiction suggest that she has become quite______them.
(A) reflective about
(B) enamored of
(C) skeptical of
(D) encouraged by
(E) offended by

7. If duty is the natural______of one's ______the course of future events, then people who are powerful have duty placed on them whether they like it or not.
(A) correlate...understanding of
(B) outgrowth....control over
(C) determinant...involvement in
(D) mitigant...preoccupation with
(E) arbiter...responsibility for

笔 记 区

BBBBAEA

Exercise 31

1. The Chinese, who began systematic astronomical and weather observations shortly after the ancient Egyptians, were assiduous record-keepers, and because of this, can claim humanity's longest continuous _____ of natural events.
   (A) defiance
   (B) documentation
   (C) maintenance
   (D) theory
   (E) domination

2. Although the discovery of antibiotics led to great advances in clinical practice, it did not represent a _______ bacterial illness, for there are some bacteria that cannot be _________ treated with antibiotics.
   (A) breakthrough in...consistently
   (B) panacea for...effectively
   (C) neglect of...efficiently
   (D) reexamination of...conventionally
   (E) resurgence of...entirely

3. Many industries are so ________ by the impact of government sanctions, equipment failure, and foreign competition that they are beginning to rely on industrial psychologists to_________ what remains of employee morale.
   (A) estranged...guard
   (B) beleaguered...salvage
   (C) overruled...undermine
   (D) encouraged...determine
   (E) restrained...confirm

4. A human being is quite _________ creature, for the gloss of rationality that covers his or her fears and _________ is thin and often easily breached.
   (A) a logical...problems

笔 记 区

(B) a frail...insecurity

(C) a valiant...phobias

(D) an ambitious...morality

(E) a ludicrous...laughter

5. The current demand for quality in the schools seems to ask not for the development of informed and active citizens, but for disciplined and productive workers with abilities that contribute to civic life only _______, if at all.

(A) indirectly

(B) politically

(C) intellectually

(D) sensibly

(E) sequentially

6. The popularity of pseudoscience and quack medicines in the nineteenth century suggests that people were very_______, but the gullibility of the public today makes citizens of yesterday look like hard-nosed _________

(A) cautious...educators

(B) sophisticated...realists

(C) rational...pragmatists

(D) naive...idealists

(E) credulous...skeptics 怀疑者

7. Although normally _________, Alison felt so strongly about the issue that she put aside her reserve and spoke up at the committee meeting.

(A) diffident

(B) contentious

(C) facetious

(D) presumptuous

(E) intrepid

笔 记 区

Exercise 32

1. According to the newspaper critic, the performances at the talent contest last night _______ from acceptable to excellent.
   (A) varied
   (B) receded
   (C) swept
   (P) averaged
   (E) declined

2. Candidates who oppose the present state income tax must be able to propose _______ ways to ______ the financing of state operations.
   (A) intelligent...initiate
   (B) individual...diversify
   (C) innovative...alleviate
   (D) arbitrary...maintain
   (E) alternate...continue

3. Linguists have now confirmed what experienced users of ASL—American Sign Language—have always implicitly known: ASL is a grammatically ________ language in that it is capable of expressing every possible syntactic relation.
   (A) limited
   (B) economical
   (C) complete
   (D) shifting
   (E) abstract

4. During the widespread fuel shortage, the price of gasoline was so ________ that suppliers were generally thought to be________ the consumer.
   (A) reactive...shielding
   (B) stable...blackmailing
   (C) depressed...cheating

(D) prohibitive...placating

(E) excessive...gouging

5. Experienced and proficient, Susan is a good, ________ trumpeter, her music is often more satisfying than Carol's brilliant but ________ playing.

(A) virtuoso...inimitable

(B) mediocre...eccentric

(C) competent...influential

(D) amateur...renowned

(E) reliable...erratic

6. However ________ they might be, Roman poets were bound to have some favorite earlier author whom they would ________

(A) subservient...imitate

(B) independent ...inspire

(C) original...emulate

(D) creative...admire

(E) talented...neglect

7. One virus strain that may help gene therapists cure genetic brain diseases can enter the peripheral nervous system and travel to the brain, ________ the need to inject the therapeutic virus directly into the brain.

(A) suggesting

(B) intensifying

(C) elucidating

(D) satisfying

(E) obviating

EBBCAAC
C

Exercise 33

1. Artificial light________ the respiratory activity of some microorganisms in the winter but not in the summer, in part because in the summer their respiration is already at its peak and thus cannot be ________
(A) stimulates...lessened
(B) inhibits...quickened
(C) reflects...expanded
(D) elevates...measured
(E) enhances...increased

2. Foucault's rejection of the concept of continuity in Western thought, though radical, was not unique; he had _________ in the United States who, without knowledge of his work, developed parallel ideas.
(A) critics
(B) counterparts
(C) disciples
(D) readers
(E) publishers

3. Recent research indicates that a system of particles which has apparently decayed to randomness from _________ state can be returned to that state; thus the system exhibits a kind of memory of its _________ condition.
(A) an equilibrium...lesser
(B) an ordered...earlier
(C) an unusual...settled
(D) a chaotic...last
(E) a higher...present

4. Jones was unable to recognize the contradictions in his attitudes that were obvious to everyone else; even the hint of an untruth was _________ to him, but he ________ serious trouble by always cheating on his taxes.

笔 记 区

(A) acceptable. risked
(B) exciting...averted
(C) repugnant...courted
(D) anathema...evaded
(E) tempting...hazarded

5. Despite an agreement between labor and management to keep the print and electronic media ______ developments, the details of the negotiations were ______ all but a few journalists from the major metropolitan newspapers.
(A) abreast of...disclosed to
(B) involved in...leaded to
(C) apprised of...withheld from
(D) speculating about...denied to
(E) ignorant of ...suppressed by

6. Numerous historical examples illustrate both the overriding influence that scientists' ________ have on their interpretation of data and the consequent__________of their intellectual objectivity.
(A) prejudices...impairment
(B) instruments...abandonment
(C) theories...independence
(D) conclusions...coloration
(E) suppositions...reinforcement

7. Not wishing to appear ____________, the junior member of the research group refrained from _________ any criticism of the senior members' plan for dividing up responsibility for the entire project.
(A) reluctant...evaluating
(B) inquisitive...offering
(C) presumptuous...venturing
(D) censorious...undercutting
(E) moralistic...observing

Exercise 34

1. This project is the first step in a long-range plan of research whose ________ goal, still many years off, is the creation of a new prototype.
   (A) cooperative
   (B) reasoned
   (C) original
   (D) ultimate
   (E) intentional

2. Wearing the latest fashions was exclusively the _________ of the wealthy until the 1850's, when mass production, aggressive entrepreneurs, and the availability of the sewing machine made them _________ the middle class.
   (A) aspiration...disagreeable to
   (B) vexation...superfluous for
   (C) bane...profitable to
   (D) prerogative...accessible to
   (E) obligation...popular with

3. Although supernovas are among the most _________ of cosmic events, these stellar explosions are often hard to _________, either because they are enormously far away or because they are dimmed by intervening dust and gas clouds.
   (A) remote...observe
   (B) luminous...detect
   (C) predictable...foresee
   (D) ancient...determine
   (E) violent...disregard

4. As is often the case with collections of lectures by ________ authors, the book as a whole is ________, although the individual contributions are outstanding in themselves.
   (A) different...disconnected

(B) incompetent...abysmal

(C) famous...systematic

(D) mediocre...unexciting

(E) various...coherent

5. The action and characters in a melodrama can be so immediately ________ that all observers can hiss the villain with an air of smug but enjoyable ________

(A) spurned...boredom

(B) forgotten...condescension

(C) classified...self-righteousness

(D) plausible...guilt

(E) gripping...skepticism

6. The theory of cosmic evolution states that the universe, having begun in a state of simplicity and ________, has ________ into great variety.

(A) equilibrium...modulated

(B) homogeneity...differentiated

(C) contrast...metamorphosed

(D) proportion...accelerated

(E) intelligibility...developed

7. The ________ with which the French aristocracy greeted the middle-class Rousseau was all the more ________ because he showed so little respect for them.

(A) deference...remarkable

(B) suspicion...uncanny

(C) reserve...unexpected

(D) anger...ironic

(E) appreciation...deserved

笔 记 区

ACDBABD E

Exercise 35

1. My family often found others laughable, but I learned quite early to be __________ while people were present, laughing only later at what was funny and mocking what to us seemed______.
   (A) polite...bizarre
   (B) impatient...unfortunate
   (C) facetious...enviable
   (D) wistful...extraordinary
   (E) superficial...deplorable

2. In today's world, manufacturers' innovations are easily copied and thus differences between products are usually _________; advertisers, therefore, are forced to _________ these differences in order to suggest the uniqueness of their clients' products.
   (A) crucial...downplay
   (B) minimal...reduce
   (C) slight...exaggerate
   (D) common...emphasize
   (E) intrinsic...create

3. Unfortunately, since courses in nutrition are often_________medical school curriculums. a family physician is________ to be an enlightening source of general information about diet.
   (A) questioned by...encouraged
   (B) encountered among...unable
   (C) unappreciated by...expected
   (D) neglected in...unlikely
   (E) squeezed into...intended

4. Even those siblings whose childhood was _________ familial feuding and intense rivalry for their parents' affection can nevertheless develop congenial and even

笔 记 区

________relationships with each other in their adult lives.

(A) scarred by...vitriolic

(B) dominated by...intimate

(C) filled with...truculent

(D) replete with...competitive

(E) devoid of...tolerant

5. Old age, even in cultures where it is ________, is often viewed with ________

(A) venerated...ambivalence

(B) rare...surprise

(C) ignored...condescension 屈尊 俯就

(D) feared...dismay

(E) honored...respect

6. Though feminist in its implications, Yvonne Rainer's 1974 film ________ the filmmaker's active involvement in feminist politics.

(A) preserved

(B) portrayed

(C) encouraged

(D) renewed

(E) antedated 比…早，先于

7. Though dealers insist that professional art dealers can make money in the art market, even an ________ knowledge is not enough: the art world is so fickle that stock-market prices are ________ by comparison.

(A) amateur's...sensible

(B) expert's...erratic

(C) investor's...booming

(D) insider's...predictable

(E) artist's...irrational

DEADEA&
B CB

Exercise 36

1. Because they had expected the spacecraft Voyager 2 to be able to gather data only about the planets Jupiter and Saturn, scientists were _________ the wealth of information it sent back from Neptune twelve years after leaving Earth.
   (A) disappointed in
   (B) concerned about
   (C) confident in
   (D) elated by
   (E) anxious for

2. The insecticide proved _________; by killing the weak adults of a species, it assured that the strong ones would mate among themselves and produce offspring still more _________ to its effects.
   (A) ineffective...hostile
   (B) cruel...vulnerable
   (C) feasible...susceptible
   (D) necessary...immune
   (E) counterproductive...resistant

3. Before the Second World War, academics still questioned whether the body of literature produced in the United States truly _________ a _________ literature, or whether such literature was only a provincial branch of English literature.
   (A) symbolized...local
   (B) constituted...national
   (C) defined...historical
   (D) outlined...good
   (E) captured...meaningful

4. Prior to the work of Heckel, illustrations of fish were often beautiful but rarely _________; this fact, combined with the ______ nature of most nine-teenth-century taxonomic descriptions, often kept scientists from recognizing differences between

笔 记 区

species.

(A) impressive...inaccurate

(B) realistic...detailed

(C) traditional...progressive

(D) precise...inexact

(E) distinctive...sophisticated

5. James had idolized the professor so much for so long that even after lunching with her several times he remained quite ________ in her presence and as a result, he could not really be himself.

(A) pleased

(B) disregarded

(C) heartened

(D) relaxed

(E) inhibited

6. One of archaeology's central dilemmas is how to reconstruct the ________ of complex ancient societies from meager and often _________ physical evidence.

(A) riddles...obsolete

(B) details...irrefutable

(C) intricacies...equivocal

(D) patterns...flawless

(E) configurations...explicit

7. The fortresslike facade of the Museum of Cartoon Art seems calculated to remind visitors that the comic strip is an art form that has often been_______by critics.

(A) charmed

(B) assailed

(C) unnoticed

(D) exhilarated

(E) overwhelmed

Exercise 37

1. In some cultures the essence of magic is its traditional integrity; it can be efficient only if it has been _________ without loss from primeval times to the present practitioner.
   (A) conventionalized
   (B) realized
   (C) transmitted
   (D) manipulated
   (E) aggrandized

2. Certain weeds that flourish among rice crops resist detection until maturity by ______ the seedling stage in the rice plant's life cycle, thereby remaining indistinguishable from the rice crop until the flowering stage.
   (A) deterring
   (B) displacing
   (C) augmenting
   (D) imitating
   (E) nurturing

3. In small farming communities, accident victims rarely sue or demand compensation: transforming a personal injury into a _________ someone else is viewed as an attempt to _________ responsibility for one's own actions.
   (A) conspiracy against...assume
   (B) claim against...elude
   (C) boon for...minimize
   (D) distinction for...shift
   (E) trauma for...proclaim

4. Professional photographers generally regard inadvertent surrealism in a photograph as a curse rather than a blessing; magazine photographers, in particular, consider themselves _________ to the extent that they can ___________ its presence in

笔记区

their photographs.

(A) skillful...enhance

(B) inadequate...eliminate

(C) original...demonstrate

(D) fortunate...minimize

(E) conventional...highlight

5. Although some consider forcefulness and ________ to be two traits desirable to the same degree, I think that making a violent effort is much less useful than maintaining a steady one.

(A) promptness

(B) persistence

(C) aggression

(D) skillfulness

(E) lucidity

6. The trick for Michael was to ________ his son an illusory orderliness; only alone at night, when the boy was asleep, could Michael ________ the chaos he kept hidden from his son.

(A) explore with...demonstrate

(B) conjure for...acknowledge

(C) conceal from...dispel

(D) demystify for...escape

(E) endure with...abandon

7. Literature is inevitably a ________ rather than ________ medium for the simple reason that writers interpose their own vision between the reader and reality.

(A) distorting...a neutral

(B) transparent...an opaque

(C) colorful...a drab

(D) flawless...an inexact

(E) flexible...a rigid

BCDDBCE

Exercise 38

1. If those large publishers that respond solely to popular literary trends continue to dominate the publishing market, the initial publication of new writers will depend on the writers' willingness to_________popular tastes.
(A) struggle against
(B) cater to
(C) admire
(D) flout
(E) elude

2. Copyright and patent laws attempt to encourage innovation by ensuring that inventors are paid for creative work, so it would be________if expanded protection under these laws discouraged entrepreneurial innovation by increasing fears of lawsuits.
(A) desirable
(B) coincidental
(C) ironic
(D) natural
(E) sensible

3. The widespread public shock at the news of the guilty verdict was caused partly by _________ news stories that had_________ acquittal.
(A) sensational...condemned
(B) buried...urged
(C) impartial...mentioned
(D) biased...predicted
(E) local...denounced

4. Although the young violinist's _________ performance with the orchestra demonstrated his technical competence, his uninspired style and lack of interpretive maturity labeled him as a novice musician rather than as a truly _________ performer.
(A) spectacular...conventional

笔 记 区

(B) blundering...artistic

(C) marginal...inept

(D) steady....accomplished

(E) dazzling...unskilled

5. An obvious style, easily identified by some superficial quirk, is properly_____ as a mere mannerism, whereas a complex and subtle style_____ reduction to a formula.

(A) avoided...risks

(B) decried...resists

(C) prized...withstands

(D) identified ...consists of

(E) cultivated...demands

6. Winsor McCay, the cartoonist, could draw with incredible_________: his comic strip about Little Nemo was characterized by marvelous draftsmanship and sequencing.

(A) sincerity

(B) efficiency

(C) virtuosity

(D) rapidity

(E) energy

7. Ethologists are convinced that many animals survive through learning—but learning that is _______ their genetic programming, learning as thoroughly _________ as the most instinctive of behavioral responses.

(A) superseded by...primitive

(B) compatible with...transient

(C) complementary to...familiar

(D) derived from...inventive

(E) dictated by...stereotyped

EDEABBC
D

Exercise 39

1. Nearly two-thirds of the country's mushroom crop is produced by 160 growers in a single county, the greatest__________ growers anywhere.
   (A) cause of
   (B) agreement among
   (C) indication of
   (D) interaction between
   (E) concentration of

2. Despite many decades of research on the gasification of coal, the data accumulated are not directly ______________to environmental questions; thus a new program of research specifically addressing such questions is_______
   (A) analogous...promising
   (B) transferable...contradictory
   (C) antithetical...unremarkable
   (D) applicable...warranted
   (E) pertinent...unnecessary

3. The development of containers, possibly made from bark or the skins of animals, although this is a matter of __________, allowed the extensive sharing of forage foods in prehistoric human societies.
   (A) record
   (B) fact
   (C) degree
   (D) importance
   (E) conjecture

4. Calculus, though still indispensable to science and technology, is no longer _______ ; it has an equal partner called discrete mathematics.
   (A) preeminent
   (B) pertinent

笔 记 区

(C) beneficial

(D) essential

(E) pragmatic

5. All _________ biological traits fall into one of two categories: those giving their possessors greater _________ the environment and those rendering them more independent of it.

(A) widespread...detachment from

(B) beneficial...control over

(C) successful...freedom from

(D) neutral...compatibility with

(E) harmful...advantage in

6. Unenlightened authoritarian managers rarely recognize a crucial reason for the low levels of serious conflict among members of democratically run work groups: a modicum of tolerance for dissent often prevents _________.

(A) demur

(B) schism

(C) cooperation

(D) compliance

(E) shortsightedness

7. The sea was not an ________the ________of the windmill; on the contrary, while the concept of the new invention passed quickly from seaport to seaport, it made little headway inland.

(A) element in...evolution

(B) issue in ...acceptance

(C) aid to...designers

(D) obstacle to...diffusion

(E) impediment to...creation

Exercise 40

1. The fact that a theory is _________ does not necessarily_________ its scientific truth,which must be established by unbiased controlled studies.
   (A) plausible...ensure
   (B) popular...limit
   (C) venerable...override
   (D) cohesive...undermine
   (E) cumbersome...alleviate

2. Often the difficulties of growing up in the public eye cause child prodigies to ________ the world of achievement before reaching adulthood; happily, they sometimes later return to competition and succeed brilliantly.
   (A) ridicule
   (B) conquer
   (C) retire from
   (D) antagonize
   (E) examine

3. Although strong legal remedies for nonpayment of child support are _________, the delay and expense associated with these remedies make it _________ to develop other options.
   (A) unpopular...useful
   (B) required...impossible
   (C) available...imperative
   (D) unavailing...impractical
   (E) nonexistent...ridiculous

4. The success of science is due in great part to its emphasis on________: the reliance on evidence rather than ________and the willingness to draw conclusions even when they conflict with traditional beliefs.
   (A) causality...experimentation

(B) empiricism...facts
(C) objectivity...preconceptions
(D) creativity...observation
(E) conservatism...assumptions

5. Because they have been so dazzled by the calendars and the knowledge of astronomy possessed by the Mayan civilization, some anthropologists have _________ achievements like the sophisticated carved calendar sticks of the Winnebago people.
(A) described
(B) acknowledged
(C) overlooked
(D) defended
(E) authenticated

6. Manipulating laboratory tissue cultures with hormones is one thing; using hormones to treat human beings, however, is contingent on whether hormones that ________ in the laboratory can affect _________ organisms, and in predictable ways.
(A) develop...similar
(B) succeed...simple
(C) fail...cellular
(D) work...whole
(E) reproduce...unknown

7. In response to the follies of today's commercial and political worlds, the author does not _________ inflamed indignation, but rather __________ the detachment and smooth aphoristic prose of an eighteenth-century wit.
(A) display...rails at
(B) rely on...avoids
(C) suppress...clings to
(D) express...affects
(E) resort to...spurns

CABABAB

Exercise 41

1. Contrary to the popular conception that it is powered by conscious objectivity, science often operates through error, happy accidents, ______ and persistence in spite of mistakes.
   (A) facts
   (B) controls
   (C) hunches
   (D) deductions
   (E) calculations

2. The well-trained engineer must understand fields as diverse as physics, economics, geology, and sociology;thus, an overly _________engineering curriculum should be avoided.
   (A) narrow
   (B) innovative
   (C) competitive
   (D) rigorous
   (E) academic

3. Their ________ of loyalties is first to oneself, next to kin, then to fellow tribe members, and finally to compa-triots.
   (A) merging
   (B) hierarchy
   (C) definition
   (D) judgment
   (E) cognizance

4. The idealized paintings of nature produced in the eighteenth century are evidence that the medieval _________natural settings had been _______ and that the outdoors now could be enjoyed without trepidation.
   (A) fear of...exorcised

笔记区

(B) concerns about...regained

(C) affection for...surmounted

(D) disinterest in...alleviated

(E) enthusiasm for...confronted

5. Art _________ science, but that does not mean that the artist must also be a scientist; an artist uses the fruits of science but need not _________ the theories from which they derive.

(A) precedes...anticipate

(B) incorporates...understand

(C) transcends...abandon

(D) imitates...repudiate

(E) resembles...contest

6. Because of its lack of theaters, the city came, ironically, to be viewed as an _________ theater town, and that reputation led entrepreneurs to believe that it would be _________ to build new theaters there.

(A) unprofitable...risky

(B) untapped...pointless

(C) unappreciated..difficult

(D) unlikely...appropriate

(E) unimpressed...shrewd

7. The natures of social history and lyric poetry are ________ , social history always recounting the _________ and lyric poetry speaking for unchanging human nature, that timeless essence beyond fashion and economics.

(A) predetermined...bygone

(B) antithetical...evanescent

(C) interdependent...unnoticed

(D) irreconcilable...unalterable

(E) indistinguishable...transitory

Exercise 42

1. The corporation expects only _________ increases in sales next year despite a yearlong effort to revive its retailing business.
   (A) unquestionable
   (B) sequential
   (C) modest
   (D) exaggerated
   (E) groundless

2. For more than a century, geologists have felt comfortable with the idea that geological processes, although very _________, are also _________ and so are capable of shaping the Earth, given enough time.
   (A) minute...sporadic
   (B) slow...steady
   (C) complex...discernible
   (D) unpredictable...constant
   (E) ponderous...intermittent

3. To avoid annihilation by parasites, some caterpillars are able to _______ periods of active growth by pre-maturely entering a dormant state, which is characterized by the ____________ of feeding.
   (A) curtail...suspension
   (B) foster...continuation
   (C) prevent...stimulation
   (D) mediate...synthesis
   (E) invert...simulation

4. The eradication of pollution is not merely a matter of ______, though the majestic beauty of nature is indeed an important consideration.
   (A) economics
   (B) legislation

(C) cleanliness
(D) aesthetics
(E) restoration

5. Even though the general's carefully qualified public statement could hardly be _________, some people took____________ it.
(A) respected...liberties with
(B) inoffensive...umbrage at
(C) faulted...exception to
(D) credited...potshots at
(E) dismissed...interest in

6. The _______ of gamblers' unsuccessful decision strategies is one _______ of the illusions built into games of chance in order to misguide players and take their money.
(A) distortion...outcome
(B) restriction...result
(C) maintenance...function
(D) prediction...accomplishment
(E) demonstration...prerequisite

7. The astronomer and feminist Maria Mitchell's own prodigious activity and the vigor of the Association for the Advancement of Women during the 1870's ________ any assertion that feminism was ________ in that period.
(A) exclude...thriving
(B) contradict...prospering
(C) pervade...remote
(D) buttress...dormant
(E) belie...quiescent

CABEDEE B

Exercise 43

1. By idiosyncratically refusing to dismiss an insubordinate member of his staff, the manager not only _________ established policy, but he also _________ his heretofore good chances for promotion.
   (A) instituted...bettered
   (B) recognized...protected
   (C) contravened...jeopardized
   (D) reiterated...computed
   (E) delimited...restricted

2. Thomas Paine, whose political writing was often flamboyant, was in private life a surprisingly _________ man: he lived in rented rooms, ate little, and wore drab clothes.
   (A) simple
   (B) controversial
   (C) sordid
   (D) comfortable
   (E) discourteous

3. It is _________ for a government to fail to do whatever it can to eliminate a totally _________ disease.
   (A) folly...innocuous
   (B) irresponsible...preventable
   (C) crucial...fatal
   (D) instinctive...devastating
   (E) detrimental...insignificant

4. Fashion is partly a search for a new language to discredit the old, a way in which each generation can________ its immediate predecessor and distinguish itself.
   (A) honor
   (B) repudiate

笔 记 区

(C) condone

(D) placate

(E) emulate

5. The "impostor syndrome" often afflicts those who fear that true self-disclosure will lower them in others' esteem; rightly handled, however, _________ may actually _________ one's standing.

(A) willfulness...consolidate

(B) imposture...undermine

(C) affectation...jeopardize

(D) candor...enhance

(E) mimicry...efface

6. In the midst of so many evasive comments, this forthright statement, whatever its intrinsic merit, plainly stands out as ____________

(A) a paradigm

(B) a misnomer

(C) a profundity

(D) an inaccuracy.

(E) an anomaly

7. Although a few delegates gave the opposition's suggestions a ______ response, most greeted the statement of a counterposition with ______.

(A) favorable...approval

(B) dispirited...reluctance

(C) surly...resentment

(D) halfhearted...composure

(E) vitriolic...civility

Exercise 44

1. The senator's reputation, though _________ by false allegations of misconduct, emerged from the ordeal _________.
   (A) shaken...unscathed
   (B) destroyed...intact
   (C) damaged...impaired
   (D) impugned...unclear
   (E) tarnished...sullied

2. Since 1813 reaction to Jane Austen's novels has oscillated between_________ and condescension; but in general later writers have esteemed her works more highly than did most of her literary ___________.
   (A) dismissal...admirers
   (B) adoration...contemporaries
   (C) disapproval...readers
   (D) indifference...followers
   (E) approbation...precursors

3. Unlike other creatures, who are shaped largely by their _________ environment, human beings are products of a culture accumulated over centuries, yet one that is constantly being _______ by massive infusions of new information from everywhere.
   (A) harsh...unconfirmed
   (B) surrounding...upheld
   (C) immediate...transformed
   (D) natural...mechanized
   (E) limited...superseded

4. The belief that science destroys the arts appears to be supported by historical evidence that the arts have _______only when the sciences have been _________.
   (A) declined...attacked
   (B) flourished...neglected

(C) matured...unconcerned

(D) succeeded...developed

(E) floundered...constrained

挣扎

5. The influence of the *Timaeus* among early philosophical thinkers was ________, if only because it was the sole dialogue ________ in Europe for almost 1,000 years.

(A) pervasive...available

(B) inestimable...suppressed

(C) unnoteworthy...abridged

(D) underestimated...studied

(E) circumscribed...translated

6. Scientists who are on the cutting edge of research must often violate common sense and make seem-ingly________assumptions because existing theories simply do not ________newly observed phenomena.

(A) radical...confirm

(B) vague...incorporate

(C) absurd...explain

(D) mistaken...reveal

(E) inexact...corroborate

7. Once a duckling has identified a parent, the instinctive bond becomes a powerful ________ for additional learning since, by ________ the parent, the duckling can acquire further information that is not genetically transmitted.

(A) impulse...surpassing

(B) referent...recognizing

(C) force...acknowledging

(D) inspiration...emulating

(E) channel...mimicking

笔 记 区

Exercise 45

1. Nonviolent demonstrations often create such tensions that a community that has constantly refused to _________ its injustices is forced to correct them: the injustices can no longer be ___________
   (A) acknowledge...ignored
   (B) decrease...verified
   (C) tolerate...accepted
   (D) address...eliminated
   (E) explain...discussed

2. Eric was frustrated because, although he was adept at making lies sound _______, when telling the truth, he _______ the power to make himself believed.
   (A) plausible...lacked
   (B) convincing...held
   (C) honest...found
   (D) true...acquired
   (E) logical...claimed

3. While nurturing parents can compensate for adversity, cold or inconsistent parents may ________ it.
   (A) exacerbate
   (B) neutralize
   (C) eradicate
   (D) ameliorate
   (E) relieve

4. The architects of New York's early skyscrapers, hinting here at a twelfth-century cathedral, there at a fifteenth-century palace, sought to legitimize the city's social strivings by _______ a history the city did not truly _______.
   (A) revealing...deserve
   (B) displaying...desire

(C) evoking...possess

(D) preserving...experience

(E) flouting...believe

5. She writes across generational lines, making the past so _________ that our belief that the present is the true locus of experience is undermined.

(A) complex

(B) distant

(C) vivid

(D) mysterious

(E) mundane

6. Although some of her fellow scientists _________ the unorthodox laboratory methodology that others found innovative, unanimous praise greeted her experimental results: at once pioneering and _________.

(A) ignored...untrustworthy

(B) complimented...foreseeable

(C) welcomed...mundane

(D) decried...unexceptionable

(E) attacked...inconclusive

7. Even after _________ against the _________ of popular sovereignty were included, major figures in the humanistic disciplines remained skeptical about the proposal to extend suffrage to the masses.

(A) recommendations...continuation

(B) safeguards...excesses

(C) arguments...introduction

(D) provisions...advantages

(E) laws...creation

BCEEDAD.
C

Exercise 46

1. Only by ignoring decades of mismanagement and inefficiency could investors conclude that a fresh infusion of cash would provide anything more than a ________ solution to the company's financial woes.
   (A) fair
   (B) temporary
   (C) genuine
   (D) realistic
   (E) complete

2. No computer system is immune to a virus, a particularly malicious program that is designed to ________ and electronically ________ the disks on which data are stored.
   (A) prepare...improve
   (B) restore...disable
   (C) infect...damage
   (D) preserve...secure
   (E) invade...repair

3. In retrospect, Gordon's students appreciated her ________ assignments, realizing that such assignments were specifically designed to ________ original thought rather than to review the content of her course.
   (A) didactic...ingrain
   (B) intimidating...thwart
   (C) difficult...discourage
   (D) conventional...explicate
   (E) enigmatic...stimulate

4. Dominant interests often benefit most from ________ of governmental interference in business, since they are able to take care of themselves if left alone.
   (A) intensification

(B) authorization

(C) centralization

(D) improvisation

(E) elimination

5. Even though political editorializing was not _________ under the new regime, journalists still experienced _______, though perceptible, governmental pressure to limit dissent.

(A) restricted...clear

(B) encouraged...strong

(C) forbidden...discreet

(D) commended...overt

(E) permitted...regular

6. It is no accident that most people find Davis' book disturbing, for it is ________ to undermine a number of beliefs they have long _________.

(A) calculated...cherished

(B) annotated...assimilated

(C) intended...denied

(D) anxious...misunderstood

(E) reputed...anticipated

7. Just as the authors' book on eels is often a key text for courses in marine vertebrate zoology, their ideas on animal development and phylogeny _________ teaching in this area.

(A) prevent

(B) defy

(C) replicate

(D) inform

(E) use

Exercise 47

1. What is most important to the monkeys in the sanctuary is that they are a group; this is so because primates are inveterately _______ and build their lives around each other.
(A) independent
(B) stable
(C) curious
(D) social
(E) proprietary

2. Although Harry Stack Sullivan is one of the most influential social scientists of this century, his ideas are now so _______ in our society that they seem almost _______
(A) novel...antiquated
(B) revolutionary...fundamental
(C) commonplace ...banal
(D) disputed...esoteric
(E) obscure...familiar

3. Given the failure of independent laboratories to replicate the results of Dr. Johnson's experiment, only the most _______ supporters of her hypothesis would be foolish enough to claim that it had been adequately _______
(A) fastidious...defined
(B) partisan...verified
(C) vigilant...publicized
(D) enlightened...researched
(E) fervent...undermined

4. A number of writers who once greatly _______ the literary critic have recently recanted, substituting _______ for their former criticism.
(A) lauded...censure

笔 记 区

(B) influenced...analysis

(C) simulated...ambivalence

(D) disparaged...approbation

(E) honored...adulation

5. In their preface, the collection's editors plead that certain of the important articles they ____________ were published too recently for inclusion, but in the case of many such articles, this _________ is not valid.

(A) discussed...replacement

(B) omitted...excuse

(C) revised...clarification

(D) disparaged...justification

(E) ignored...endorsement

6. Word order in a sentence was much freer in old French than it is in French today, this _______disappeared as the French language gradually lost its case distinctions.

(A) restriction

(B) license

(C) similarity

(D) rigidity

(E) imperative

7. The actual _________ of Wilson's position was always ________by his refusal to compromise after having initially agreed to negotiate a settlement.

(A) outcome...foreshadowed

(B) logic...enhanced

(C) rigidity...betrayed

(D) uncertainty...alleviated

(E) cowardice...highlighted

笔 记 区

Exercise 48

1. Even though formidable winters are the norm in the Dakotas, many people were unprepared for the _________ of the blizzard of 1888.
   (A) inevitability
   (B) ferocity
   (C) importance
   (D) probability
   (E) mildness

2. Congress is having great difficulty developing a consensus on energy policy, primarily because the policy objectives of various members of Congress rest on such _________assumptions.
   (A) commonplace
   (B) trivial
   (C) explicit
   (D) divergent
   (E) fundamental

3. Salazar's presence in the group was so _____ the others that they lost most of their earlier ______; failure, for them, became all but unthinkable.
   (A) reassuring to ...trepidation
   (B) unnoticed by...curiosity
   (C) unusual to...harmony
   (D) endearing to...confidence
   (E) unexpected by...exhilaration

4. In sharp contrast to the intense _________ of the young republic, with its utopian faith in democracy and hopes for eternal human progress, recent developments suggest a mood of almost unrelieved ________
   (A) idealism...cynicism
   (B) individualism...escapism

(C) sectarianism...recklessness

(D) assertiveness...ambition

(E) righteousness...egalitarianism

5. Although the passage of years has softened the initially hostile reaction to his poetry, even now only a few independent observers _________ his works.

(A) praise

(B) revile

(C) scrutinize

(D) criticize

(E) neglect

6. Any population increase beyond a certain level necessitates greater ________ vegetable foods; thus, the ability of a society to choose meat over cereals always arises, in part, from ________ the number of people.

(A) reliance on...replenishing

(B) production of...estimating

(C) spending on...concealing

(D) recourse to...limiting

(E) attention to...varying

7. Whereas biologists must maintain a _____attitude toward the subjects of their research, social scientists must, paradoxically, combine personal involvement and scholarly _____.

(A) scrupulous...sympathy

(B) careful...abandon

(C) casual...precision

(D) passive...passion

(E) disinterested...detachment

DEECDEB
B D

Exercise 49

1. A recent survey shows that, while ninety-four percent of companies conducting management-training programs open them to women, women are ________ only seventy-four percent of those programs.
   (A) protesting against
   (B) participating in
   (C) displeased by
   (D) allowed in
   (E) refused by

2. This poetry is not ________; it is more likely to appeal to an international audience than is poetry with strictly regional themes.
   (A) familiar
   (B) democratic
   (C) technical
   (D) complex
   (E) provincial

3. Although the architect's concept at first sounded too _____ to be ____ , his careful analysis of every aspect of the project convinced the panel that the proposed building was indeed, structurally feasible.
   (A) mundane...attractive
   (B) eclectic...appealing
   (C) grandiose...affordable
   (D) innovative...ignored
   (E) visionary...practicable

4. Dramatic literature often ________ the history of a culture in that it takes as its subject matter the important events that have shaped and guided the culture.
   (A) confounds
   (B) repudiates

笔 记 区

(C) recapitulates

(D) anticipates

(E) polarizes

5. It was her view that the country's problems had been________ by foreign technocrats, so that to invite them to come back would be counterproductive.

(A) foreseen

(B) attacked

(C) ascertained

(D) exacerbated

(E) analyzed

6. Unlike the easily studied neutral and ionized ________ that compose the primary disk of the Milky Way itself, the components of the _________ surrounding our galaxy have proved more resistant to study.

(A) figments...envelope

(B) essences...fluctuations

(C) elements...problems

(D) calculations...perimeter

(E) materials...region

7. Their _______ was expressed in quotidian behavior: they worshipped regularly, ______ all the regenerative processes of nature respect, and even awe.

(A) selflessness...reserving to

(B) moderation...extending to

(C) reverence...exacting from

(D) piety...according

(E) serenity...refusing

CDAADDC
E

Exercise 50

1. Exposure to low-intensity gamma radiation slows the rate of growth of the spoilage microorganisms in food in much the same way that the low heat used in pasteurization ________ the spoilage action of the microorganisms in milk.
(A) precludes
(B) initiates
(C) inhibits
(D) isolates
(E) purifies

2. It is difficult to distinguish between the things that charismatic figures do ________ and those that are carefully contrived for effect.
(A) formally
(B) publicly
(C) prolifically
(D) spontaneously
(E) willfully

3. A misconception frequently held by novice writers is that sentence structure mirrors thought: the more convoluted the structure, the more ________ the ideas.
(A) complicated
(B) inconsequential
(C) elementary
(D) fanciful
(E) blatant

4. He was regarded by his followers, as something of ________, not only because of his insistence on strict discipline, but also because of his ________ adherence to formal details. 严格执行纪律的人
(A) a martinet...rigid
(B) an authority...sporadic

笔 记 区

(C) a tyrant...reluctant

(D) a fraud...conscientious

(E) an acolyte...maniacal 发狂的 助手

5. The techniques now available to livestock breeders will continue to be ________, but will probably be ________ by new ones under development.

(A) fruitful...reversed

(B) refined...upgraded

(C) inconvenient...reassessed

(D) used...supplemented

(E) harmless...improved

6. Unlike philosophers who constructed theoretically ideal states, she built a theory based on ________; thus, although her constructs may have been inelegant, they were ________ sound.

(A) reality...aesthetically

(B) intuition...intellectually

(C) surmise...scientifically

(D) experience...empirically

(E) conjecture...factually

7. The chances that a species will ________ are reduced if any vital function is restricted to a single kind of organ; ________ by itself possesses an enormous survival advantage.

(A) degenerate...complexity

(B) expire...size

(C) disappear...variety

(D) flourish...symmetry

(E) persist...redundancy

笔 记 区

Exercise 51

1. Read's apology to Heflin was not exactly abject and did little to _____ their decades-long quarrel, which had been as _____ as the academic etiquette of scholarly journals permitted.
(A) encourage...sporadic
(B) dampen...courteous
(C) obscure...ceremonious
(D) resolve...acrimonious
(E) blur...sarcastic

2. The technical know-how, if not the political _________ ,appears already at hand to feed the world's exploding population and so to _______ at last the ancient scourges of malnutrition and famine.
(A) will...weaken
(B) expertise...articulate
(C) doubt...banish
(D) power...denounce
(E) commitment...eradicate

3. While not _________ with the colorfully obvious forms of life that are found in a tropical rain forest, the desert is _________ to a surprisingly large number of species.
(A) brimming...foreign
(B) endowed...detrimental
(C) imbued...hostile
(D) teeming...host
(E) confronted...home

4. Roman historians who study the period 30 B.C. to A.D. 180 can _________ the "Augustan peace" only by failing to recognize that this peace in many respects resembled that of death.

笔 记 区

(A) decry
(B) applaud
(C) ridicule
(D) demand
(E) disprove

5. Although ________ is usually thought to spring from regret for having done something wrong, it may be that its origin is the realization that one's own nature is irremediably ________.
(A) contrition...resilient
(B) certitude...confident
(C) skepticism...innocent
(D) remorse...flawed
(E) resignation...frivolous

6. The labor union and the company's management, despite their long history of unfailingly acerbic disagreement on nearly every issue, have nevertheless reached an unexpectedly ________, albeit still tentative, agreement on next year's contract.
(A) swift
(B) onerous
(C) hesitant
(D) reluctant
(E) conclusive

7. Marshall's confrontational style could alienate almost anyone: he even antagonized a board of directors that included a number of his supporters and that had a reputation for not being easily ________
(A) intimidated
(B) mollified
(C) reconciled
(D) provoked
(E) motivated

Exercise 52

1. Paradoxically, England's colonization of North America was _______ by its success: the increasing prosperity of the colonies diminished their dependence upon, and hence their loyalty to, their home country.
(A) demonstrated
(B) determined
(C) altered
(D) undermined
(E) distinguished

2. To believe that a culture's achievement can be measured by the _________ of its written material requires one to accept that a page of junk mail is as _________ as a page of great literature.
(A) nature...readable
(B) quality...prevalent
(C) timelessness...understandable
(D) applicability...eloquent
(E) volume...valuable

3. The valedictory address, as it has developed in American colleges and universities over the years, has become a very strict form, a literary _________ that permits very little_________.
(A) text...clarity
(B) work...tradition
(C) genre...deviation
(D) oration...grandiloquence
(E) achievement...rigidity

4. Poe's _________ reviews of contemporary fiction, which often find great merit in otherwise ________ literary gems, must make us respect his critical judgment in addition to his well-known literary talent.

笔 记 区

(A) thorough...completed

易怒的 (B) petulant...unpopular

(C) insightful...unappreciated

(D) enthusiastic...acclaimed

(E) harsh...undeserving

5. Actual events in the history of life on Earth are accidental in that any outcome embodies just one _______ among millions; yet each out come can be _______ interpreted.

(A) coincidence...randomly

(B) relationship...predictably

(C) fact ...readily

(D) happening...uniquely

(E)possibility...rationally

6. If efficacious new medicines have side effects that are commonly observed and _____, such medicines are too often considered _____, even when laboratory tests suggest caution.

(A) unremarkable...safe

(B) unpredictable...reliable

(C) frequent...outdated

(D) salutary...experimental

(E) complicated...useful

7. From the outset, the concept of freedom of the seas from the proprietary claims of nations was challenged by a contrary notion—that of the ________ of the oceans for reasons of national security and profit.

(A) promotion

(B) exploration

(C) surveying

(D) conservation

(E) enclosure

Exercise 53

1. Having sufficient income of her own constituted for Alice________ independence that made possible a degree of________ in her emotional life as well.
   (A) a material...security
   (B) a profound...conformity
   (C) a financial...economy
   (D) a psychological...extravagance
   (E) an unexpected...uncertainty

2. Doreen justifiably felt she deserved recognition for the fact that the research institute had been ________a position of preeminence, since it was she who had ________ the transformation.
   (A) reduced to...controlled
   (B) raised to...observed
   (C) mired in...imagined
   (D) maintained in...created
   (E) returned to...directed

3. Experienced employers recognize that business students who can ________ different points of view are ultimately more effective as managers than are the brilliant and original students who ________ dogmatically to their own formulations.
   (A) discredit...revert
   (B) assimilate...adhere
   (C) impose...refer
   (D) disregard...incline
   (E) advocate...relate

4. Under ethical guidelines recently adopted by the National Institutes of Health, human genes are to be manipulated only to correct diseases for which ________ treatments are unsatisfactory.
   (A) similar

(B) most

(C) dangerous

(D) uncommon

(E) alternative

5. Some paleontologists debate whether the diversity of species has _________ since the Cambrian period, or whether imperfections in the fossil record only suggest greater diversity today, while in actuality there has been either____________ or decreased diversity.

(A) changed...escalation

(B) increased...stasis

(C) expanded...discontinuity

(D) declined...reduction

(E) improved...deviation

6. Imposing steep fines on employers for on-the-job injuries to workers could be an effective _________ to creating a safer workplace, especially in the case of employers with poor safety records.

(A) antidote

(B) alternative

(C) addition

(D) deterrent

(E) incentive

7. The _________ costumes of Renaissance Italy, with their gold and silver embroidery and figured brocades. were the antithesis of Spanish _________, with its dark muted colors, plain short capes, and high collars edged with small ruffs.

(A) striking...obliqueness

(B) extravagant...profligacy

(C) austere...informality

(D) unpretentious...asceticism

(E) sumptuous...sobriety

Exercise 54

1. Though environmentalists have targeted some herbicides as potentially dangerous, the manu-facturers, to the environmentalists' dismay, ________the use of these herbicides on lawns.
   (A) defy
   (B) defer
   (C) defend
   (D) assail
   (E) disparage

2. The transition from the Paleolithic to the Neolithic era is viewed by most art historians as a ____, because, instead of an increasingly ______ pictorial art, we find degeneration.
   (A) milestone...debased
   (B) consolidation...diverse
   (C) calamity...aberrant
   (D) regression...sophisticated
   (E) continuation...improved

3. There are, as yet, no vegetation types or ecosystems whose study has been_________ to the extent that they no longer_________ ecologists.
   (A) perfected...hinder
   (B) exhausted...interest
   (C) prolonged...require
   (D) prevented...challenge
   (E) delayed...benefit

4. Always circumspect, she was reluctant to make judgments, but once arriving at a conclusion, she was ________ in its defense.
   (A) nonplussed
   (B) obsequious

(C) intransigent

(D) deferential

(E) negligent

5. Marison was a scientist of unusual _______ and imagination who had startling success in ____________ new and fundamental principles well in advance of their general recognition.

(A) restiveness...acknowledging

(B) precision...coordinating

(C) aggression...resisting

(D) candor...dispelling

(E) insight...discerning

6. Aptly enough, this work so imbued with the notion of changing times and styles has been constantly ________over the years, thereby reflecting its own mutability.

(A) appreciated

(B) emulated

(C) criticized

(D) revised

(E) reprinted

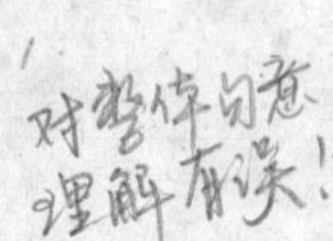

7. Human nature and long distances have made exceeding the speed limit a ________ tradition in the state, so the legislators surprised no one when, acceding to public practice, they ________ increased penalties for speeding.

(A) disquieting...endorsed

(B) long-standing...considered

(C) controversial...suggested

(D) cherished...rejected

(E) hallowed...investigated

Exercise 55

1. Contrary to the antiquated idea that the eighteenth century was a _________ island of elegant assurance, evidence reveals that life for most people was filled with uncertainty and insecurity.
(A) clannish
(B) declining
(C) tranquil
(D) recognized
(E) sprawling

2. The disjunction between educational objectives that stress independence and individuality and those that emphasize obedience to rules and cooperation with others reflects a________ that arises from the values on which these objectives are based.
(A) conflict
(B) redundancy
(C) gain
(D) predictability
(E) wisdom

3. In scientific studies, supporting evidence is much more satisfying to report than are discredited hypotheses, but, in fact, the _______ of errors is more likely to be ________ than is the establishment of probable truth.
(A) formulation...permitted
(B) correction...ignored
(C) detection...useful
(D) accumulation...agreeable
(E) refinement...conditional

4. Many more eighteenth-century novels were written by women than by men, but this dominance has, until very recently, been regarded merely as _________ fact, a bit

笔 记 区

of arcane knowledge noted only by bibliographers.

(A) a controversial

(B) a statistical

(C) an analytical

(D) an explicit

(E) an unimpeachable 无可指责的

5. Although Tom was aware that it would be ________ to display annoyance publicly at the sales conference, he could not ____________ his irritation with the client's unreasonable demands.

(A) inadvisable...evince

(B) efficacious...suppress

(C) pragmatic...counter

(D) captious...express

(E) impolitic...hide

6. The pungent verbal give-and-take among the characters makes the novel ________ reading, and this very _________ suggests to me that some of the opinions voiced may be the author's.

(A) disturbing...flatness

(B) tedious...inventiveness

(C) lively...spiritedness

(D) necessary...steadiness

(E) rewarding...frivolousness

7. He felt it would be _________, in view of the intense _________ that would likely follow, to make the sacrifice required in order to gain such little advantage.

(A) charitable...growth

(B) welcomed...prejudice

(C) futile...encouragement

(D) academic...acclaim

(E) unrealistic...turmoil

笔 记 区

Exercise 56

1. A good doctor knows that knowledge about medicine will continue to _______ and that, therefore, formal professional training can never be an_________ guide to good practice.
   (A) vary...adaptable
   (B) change...absolute
   (C) ossify...inflexible
   (D) pertain...invaluable
   (E) intensify...obsolescent

2. Because many of the minerals found on the ocean floor are still _________ on land, where mining is relatively inexpensive, mining the ocean floor has yet to become a _________ enterprise.
   (A) scarce...common
   (B) accessible...marginal
   (C) unidentified...subsidized
   (D) conserved...public
   (E) plentiful...profitable

3. In certain forms of discourse such as the parable, the central point of a message can be effectively communicated even though this point is not _________.
   (A) preferred
   (B) explicit
   (C) inferable
   (D) discerned
   (E) illustrated

4. Gould claimed no ______ knowledge of linguistics, but only a hobbyist's interest in language.
   (A) manifest
   (B) plausible

(C) technical
(D) rudimentary
(E) insignificant

5. The legislators of 1563 realized the ________ of trying to regulate the flow of labor without securing its reasonable remuneration, and so the second part of the statute dealt with establishing wages.
(A) intricacy
(B) anxiety
(C) futility
(D) necessity
(E) decadence

6. The Gibsons were little given to ________ in any form; not one of them was afraid of ________, of being and seeming unlike their neighbors.
(A) humility...absurdity
(B) excellence...mediocrity
(C) anger...confrontation
(D) conformism...singularity
(E) ostentation...eccentricity

7. Carruthers' latest literary criticism ________ her reputation for trenchant commentary; despite its intriguing title and the fulsome praise on its dust jacket, it is nothing more than a collection of ________
(A) reinforces...pronouncements
(B) belies...platitudes
(C) prejudices...insights
(D) advances...aphorisms
(E) undermines...judgments

DECADEC
C BCD

Exercise 57

1. Since most if not all learning occurs through______, relating one observation to another, it would be strange indeed if the study of other cultures did not also illuminate the study of our own.
(A) assumptions
(B) experiments
(C) comparisons
(D) repetitions
(E) impressions

2. The acts of vandalism that these pranksters had actually ______ were insignificant compared with those they had ______ but had not attempted.
(A) hidden ...renounced
(B) advocated ...meditated
(C) inflicted ...dismissed
(D) committed ...effected
(E) perpetrated ...contemplated

3. Many of her followers remain ______ to her, and even those who have rejected her leadership are unconvinced of the ______ of replacing her during the current turmoil.
(A) opposed...urgency
(B) friendly...harm
(C) loyal...wisdom
(D) cool...usefulness
(E) sympathetic...disadvantage

4. Although Simpson was ingenious at ______ to appear innovative and spontaneous, beneath the ruse he remained uninspired and rigid in his approach to problem-solving.
(A) intending

笔 记 区

(B) contriving
(C) forbearing
(D) declining
(E) deserving

5. Although just barely ______ as a writer of lucid prose, Jones was an extremely ______ editor who worked superbly with other writers in helping them improve the clarity of their writing.
(A) deficient...muddling
(B) proficient...contentious
(C) adequate...capable
(D) appalling...competent
(E) engaging...inept

6. By ______ scientific rigor with a quantitative approach, researchers in the social sciences may often have ______ their scope to those narrowly circumscribed topics that are well suited to quantitative methods.
(A) undermining...diminished
(B) equating...enlarged
(C) vitiating...expanded
(D) identifying...limited
(E) imbuing...broadened

7. The failure of many psychotherapists to ______ the results of pioneering research could be due in part to the specialized nature of such findings: even ______ findings may not be useful.
(A) understand...baffling
(B) envision...accessible
(C) utilize...momentous
(D) reproduce...duplicated
(E) affirm...controversial

笔 记 区

EDABEEC
B

Exercise 58

1. In the nineteenth century, novelists and unsympathetic travelers portrayed the American West as a land of______ adversity, whereas promoters and idealists created ______ image of a land of infinite promise.
(A) lurid...a mundane
(B) incredible...an underplayed
(C) dispiriting...an identical
(D) intriguing...a luxuriant
(E) unremitting...a compelling

2. Although the mental process that creates a fresh and original poem or drama is doubtless ______ that which originates and elaborates scientific discoveries, there is clearly a discernible difference between the creators.
(A) peripheral to
(B) contiguous with
(C) opposed to
(D) analogous to
(E) inconsistent with

3. Joe spoke of superfluous and ______ matters with exactly the same degree of intensity, as though for him serious issues mattered neither more nor less than did ______.
(A) vital...trivialities
(B) redundant...superficialities
(C) important...necessities
(D) impractical...outcomes
(E) humdrum...essentials

4. Before adapting to changes in values, many prefer to ______, to ______ the universally agreed-on principles that have been upheld for centuries.
(A) innovate ...protect

笔 记 区

(B) resist ...defend

(C) ponder ...subvert

(D) vacillate ...publicize

(E) revert ...ignore

5. Those who fear the influence of television deliberately________ its persuasive power, hoping that they might keep knowledge of its potential to effect social change from being widely disseminated.

(A) promote

(B) underplay 淡化

(C) excuse

(D) laud

(E) suspect

6. He had expected gratitude for his disclosure, but instead he encountered ______ bordering on hostility.

(A) patience

(B) discretion

(C) openness

(D) ineptitude

(E) indifference

7. Although Irish literature continued to flourish after the sixteenth century, a ______ tradition is ______ in the visual arts: we think about Irish culture in terms of the word, not in terms of pictorial images.

(A) rich...superfluous

(B) lively...found

(C) comparable...absent

(D) forgotten...apparent

(E) lost...extant

CEBAEA&C D

Exercise 59

1. A computer program can provide information in ways that force students to ___ learning instead of being merely ______ of knowledge.
(A) shore up ...reservoirs
(B) accede to ...consumers
(C) participate in ...recipients
(D) compensate for...custodians
(E) profit from ...beneficiaries

2. Perhaps because scientists have been so intrigued by dogs' superior senses of smell and hearing, researchers have long ______ their eyesight, assuming that they inhabit a drab, black-and-white world, devoid of color.
(A) studied
(B) coveted
(C) appreciated
(D) resented
(E) underestimated

3. In contrast to the substantial muscular activity required for inhalation, exhalation is usually a ______ process.
(A) slow
(B) passive
(C) precise
(D) complex
(E) conscious

4. Unlike many recent interpretations of Beethoven's piano sonatas, the recitalist's performance was a delightfully free and introspective one; nevertheless, it was also, seemingly paradoxically, quite ______.
(A) appealing
(B) exuberant

笔 记 区

(C) idiosyncratic

(D) unskilled

(E) controlled

5. The children's ______ natures were in sharp contrast to the even-tempered dispositions of their parents.

(A) mercurial

(B) blithe

(C) phlegmatic

(D) introverted

(E) artless

6. The accusations we bring against others should be______ ourselves; they should not ______ complacency and easy judgments on our part concerning our own moral conduct.

(A) definitions of...produce

(B) instructions to...equate

(C) denigrations of...exclude

(D) warnings to...justify

(E) parodies of...satirize

7. The diplomat, selected for her demonstrated patience and skill in conducting such delicate negotiations, ______ to make a decision during the talks because any sudden commitment at that time would have been ______.

(A) resolved...detrimental

(B) refused...apropos

(C) declined...inopportune

(D) struggled...unconscionable

(E) hesitated...warranted

Exercise 60

1. It is assumed that scientists will avoid making ______ claims about the results of their experiments because of the likelihood that they will be exposed when other researchers cannot ______ their findings.
   (A) hypothetical...evaluate
   (B) fraudulent...duplicate
   (C) verifiable...contradict
   (D) radical...contest
   (E) extravagant...dispute

2. The new ______ of knowledge has created ______ people: everyone believes that his or her subject cannot and possibly should not be understood by others.
   (A) specialization...barriers between
   (B) decline...associations among
   (C) redundancy...complacency in
   (D) disrepute...concern for
   (E) promulgation...ignorance among

3. One theory about intelligence sees ______ as the logical structure underlying thinking and insists that since animals are mute, they must be ______ as well.
   (A) behavior...inactive
   (B) instinct...cooperative
   (C) heredity...thoughtful
   (D) adaptation...brutal
   (E) language...mindless

4. The President reached a decision only after lengthy ________, painstakingly weighing the ______ opinions expressed by cabinet members.
   (A) deliberation...divergent
   (B) confrontation...unanimous
   (C) relegation...consistent

(D) speculation...conciliatory

(E) canvassing...arbitrary

5. Once Renaissance painters discovered how to ______ volume and depth, they were able to replace the medieval convention of symbolic, two-dimensional space with the more ______ illusion of actual space.

(A) reverse...conventional

(B) portray...abstract

(C) deny...concrete

(D) adumbrate...fragmented

(E) render...realistic

6. High software prices are frequently said to ________ widespread illegal copying, although the opposite — that high prices are the cause of the copying — is equally plausible.

(A) contribute to

(B) result from

(C) correlate with

(D) explain

(E) precede

7. As early as the seventeenth century, philosophers called attention to the ______ character of the issue, and their twentieth-century counterparts still approach it with ______.

(A) absorbing...indifference

(B) unusual...composure

(C) complex...antipathy

(D) auspicious...caution

(E) problematic...uneasiness

笔 记 区

ECBACEE
D

Exercise 61

1. Although sales have continued to increase since last April, unfortunately the rate of increase has ______.
   (A) resurged
   (B) capitulated
   (C) retaliated
   (D) persevered
   (E) decelerated

2. As long as the nuclear family is ______ a larger kinship group through contiguous residence on undivided land, the pressure to ______ and thus to get along with relatives is strong.
   (A) nurtured among...abstain
   (B) excluded from...compromise
   (C) embedded in ...share
   (D) scattered throughout...reject
   (E) accepted by ...lead

3. If a species of parasite is to survive, the host organisms must live long enough for the parasite to ______ ; if the host species becomes______, so do its parasites.
   (A) atrophy...healthy
   (B) reproduce...extinct
   (C) disappear...widespread
   (D) succumb...nonviable
   (E) mate...infertile

4. Though ______ in her personal life, Edna St. Vincent Millay was nonetheless ______ about her work, usually producing several pages of complicated rhyme in a day.
   (A) jaded...feckless 没有价值的
   (B) verbose...ascetic

笔 记 区

(C) vain...humble

易冲动的(D) impulsive...disciplined

(E) self-assured...sanguine

5. Although Georgia O'Keeffe is best known for her affinity with the desert landscape, her paintings of urban subjects ______ her longtime residency in New York City.

(A) condemn

(B) obfuscate

(C) attest to

(D) conflict with

(E) contend with

6. Schlesinger has recently assumed a conciliatory attitude that is not ______ by his colleagues, who continue to ______ compromise.

(A) eschewed...dread

(B) shared...defend

(C) questioned...reject

(D) understood...advocate

(E) commended...disparage

7. Although the meanings of words may necessarily be liable to change, it does not follow that the lexicographer is therefore unable to render spelling, in a great measure, ______

(A) arbitrary

(B) superfluous

(C) interesting

(D) flexible

(E) constant

笔记区

Exercise 62

1. Though ______ to some degree, telling a small lie sometimes enables one to avoid ______ another's feelings.
   (A) necessary...mollifying
   (B) regrettable...harming
   (C) unfortunate...exaggerating
   (D) attractive...considering
   (E) difficult...resisting

2. Given her previously expressed interest and the ambitious tone of her recent speeches, the senator's attempt to convince the public that she is not interested in running for a second term is ______.
   (A) laudable
   (B) likely
   (C) authentic
   (D) futile
   (E) sincere

3. Despite a string of dismal earnings reports, the two-year-old strategy to return the company to profitability is beginning to ______.
   (A) falter
   (B) disappoint
   (C) compete
   (D) work
   (E) circulate

4. The value of Davis' sociological research is compromised by his unscrupulous tendency to use materials______ in order to substantiate his own claims, while ______ information that points to other possible conclusions.
   (A) haphazardly...deploying
   (B) selectively...disregarding

(C) cleverly...weighing
(D) modestly...refuting
(E) arbitrarily...emphasizing

5. She was criticized by her fellow lawyers not because she was not ______, but because she so ______ prepared her cases that she failed to bring the expected number to trial.
(A) well versed...knowledgeably
(B) well trained...enthusiastically
(C) congenial...rapidly
(D) hardworking...minutely
(E) astute...efficiently

6. Because the high seriousness of their narratives resulted in part from their metaphysics, Southern writers were praised for their ______ bent.
(A) technical
(B) discursive
(C) hedonistic
(D) philosophical
(E) scientific

7. The National Archives contain information so ______ that researchers have been known never to publish because they cannot bear to bring their studies to an end.
(A) divisive
(B) seductive
(C) selective
(D) repetitive
(E) resourceful

Exercise 63

1. Some activists believe that because the health-care system has become increasingly______ to those it serves, individuals must ______ bureaucratic impediments in order to develop and promote new therapies.
   (A) attuned...avoid
   (B) inimical...utilize
   (C) unresponsive ...circumvent
   (D) indifferent...supplement
   (E) sensitized...forsake

2. Honeybees tend to be more ______ than earth bees: the former, unlike the latter, search for food together and signal their individual findings to one another.
   (A) insular
   (B) aggressive
   (C) differentiated
   (D) mobile
   (E) social

3. It is disappointing to note that the latest edition of the bibliography belies its long-standing reputation for ______ by ______ some significant references to recent publications.
   (A) imprecision...appropriating
   (B) relevance...adding
   (C) timeliness...updating
   (D) meticulousness...revising
   (E) exhaustiveness...omitting

4. The author argues for serious treatment of such arts as crochet and needlework, finding in too many art historians a cultural blindness _____ to their ______ textiles as a medium in which women artists predominate.
   (A) traceable...prejudice against

(B) opposed...distrust of
(C) referring...need for
(D) reduced...respect for
(E) corresponding...expertise in

5. Species with relatively ______ metabolic rates, including hibernators, generally live longer than those whose metabolic rates are more rapid.
(A) prolific
(B) sedentary
(C) sluggish
(D) measured
(E) restive

6. Even though the survey was designated as an interdisciplinary course, it involved no real ______ of subject matter.
(A) encapsulation
(B) organization
(C) synthesis
(D) discussion
(E) verification

7. Far from being ______, Pat was always ______ to appear acquiescent.
(A) unctuous...loath
(B) brazen...reluctant
(C) ignoble...concerned
(D) obsequious...eager
(E) gregarious...willing

BEBCDEB A

Exercise 64

1. Because the monkeys under study are ______ the presence of human beings, they typically ______ human observers and go about their business
   (A) ambivalent about ...welcome
   (B) habituated to ...disregard
   (C) pleased with ...snub
   (D) inhibited by ...seek
   (E) unaware of ...avoid

2. The form and physiology of leaves vary according to the ______ in which they develop: for example, leaves display a wide range of adaptations to different degrees of light and moisture.
   (A) relationship
   (B) species
   (C) sequence
   (D) patterns
   (E) environment

3. Though one cannot say that Michelangelo was an impractical designer, he was, of all nonprofessional architects known, the most ______ in that he was the least constrained by tradition or precedent.
   (A) pragmatic
   (B) adventurous
   (C) empirical
   (D) skilled
   (E) learned

4. The documentary film about high school life was so realistic and ______ that feelings of nostalgia flooded over the college-age audience.
   (A) logical
   (B) pitiful

(C) evocative

(D) critical

(E) clinical

5. Although the records of colonial New England are ______ in comparison with those available in France or England, the records of other English colonies in America are even more ______.

   (A) sporadic...irrefutable

   (B) sparse...incontrovertible

   (C) ambiguous...authoritative

   (D) sketchy...fragmentary

   (E) puzzling ...unquestionable

6. Belying his earlier reputation for ______ as a negotiator, Morgan had recently assumed a more ______ stance for which many of his erstwhile critics praised him.

   (A) intransigence...conciliatory

   (B) impropriety...intolerant

   (C) inflexibility...unreasonable

   (D) success...authoritative

   (E) incompetence...combative

7. Because early United States writers thought that the mark of great literature was grandiosity and elegance not to be found in common speech, they ______ the vernacular.

   (A) dissected

   (B) avoided

   (C) misunderstood

   (D) investigated

   (E) exploited

Exercise 65

1. Her lecture gave a sense of how empty the universe is, in spite of the ______ number of stars within it.
(A) diminishing
(B) varying
(C) enormous
(D) unusual
(E) limited

2. He was widely regarded as a ______ man because he revealed daily his distrust of human nature and human motives.
(A) disrespectful
(B) cynical
(C) confused
(D) misinformed
(E) fanatical

3. Students of the Great Crash of 1929 have never understood why even the most informed observers did not recognize and heed the ______ economic danger signals that in ______ seem so apparent.
(A) obvious...combination
(B) early...conclusion
(C) direct...application
(D) future...potential
(E) prior...retrospect

4. It would seem that absolute qualities in art ______ us, that we cannot escape viewing works of art in ______ of time and circumstance.
(A) enlighten...a pattern
(B) frighten...an absence
(C) confuse...a welter

笔记区

(D) elude ...a context
(E) deceive...a milieu

5. Lizzie was a brave woman who could dare to incur a great danger for an adequate ______.
(A) risk
(B) combat
(C) object
(D) event
(E) encounter

6. It would be misleading to use a published play to generalize about fifteenth-century drama: the very fact of publication should serve as a ______ of the play's ______ character.
(A) qualification...unusual
(B) manifestation...unsophisticated
(C) restatement...untraditional
(D) warning...unrepresentative
(E) demonstration...unliterary

7. Human reaction to the realm of thought is often as strong as that to sensible presences; our higher moral life is based on the fact that ______ sensations actually present may have a weaker influence on our action than do ideas of ______ facts.
(A) disturbing...ordinary
(B) material...remote
(C) emotional...impersonal
(D) definitive...controversial
(E) familiar...symbolic

笔 记 区

CEDDCDC
D D

Exercise 66

1. Unlike a judge, who must act alone, a jury discusses a case and then reaches its decision as a group, thus minimizing the effect of ______ bias.
   (A) legal
   (B) professional
   (C) individual
   (D) unexpected
   (E) unarticulated

2. The wilderness is ______ in that it permits people to face an important reality—one that demands much of them as thinking, reacting, working individuals, not ______ as human machines.
   (A) foreign...necessarily
   (B) intangible...physically
   (C) stimulating...creatively
   (D) discouraging...neutrally
   (E) valuable...merely

3. Suspicious of too powerful a President, Americans nonetheless are ______ when a President does not act decisively.
   (A) unified
   (B) indifferent
   (C) content
   (D) uneasy
   (E) adamant

4. Because it has no distinct and recognizable typographical form and few recurring narrative conventions, the novel is, of all literary genres, the least susceptible to ______.
   (A) misuse
   (B) imprecision

笔 记 区

(C) inquiry

(D) definition

(E) innovation

5. For many young people during the Roaring Twenties, a disgust with the excesses of American culture ______ a wanderlust to provoke an exodus abroad.

(A) stymied

(B) overwhelmed

(C) reflected

(D) combined with

(E) conflicted with

6. Some biologists argue that each specifically human trait must have arisen gradually and erratically, and that it is therefore difficult to isolate definite______in the evolution of the species.

(A) fluctuations

(B) generations

(C) predispositions

(D) milestones

(E) manifestations

7. Certainly Murray's preoccupation with the task of editing the *Oxford English Dictionary* begot a kind of monomania, but it must be regarded as a ______ or at least an innocuous one.

(A) tame

(B) tendentious

(C) meretricious

(D) beneficent

(E) sincere

Exercise 67

1. Because its average annual rainfall is only about four inches, one of the major tasks faced by the country has been to find ______sources of water.
   (A) discontinuous
   (B) natural
   (C) supplementary
   (D) pervasive
   (E) initial

2. Even though many persons in the audience jeered the star throughout the play, she ______ curtain calls.
   (A) refused all
   (B) adored some
   (C) delayed several
   (D) appeared for
   (E) balked at

3. Despite some allowances for occupational mobility, the normal expectation of seventeenth-century English society was that the child's vocation would develop along familial lines; ______ the career of one's parents was therefore ______.
   (A) disagreement with ...forbidden
   (B) divergence from ...limited
   (C) preparation for ...difficult
   (D) reliance on ...unanticipated
   (E) assumption of ...premature

4. While admitting that the risks incurred by use of the insecticide were not ______, the manufacturer's spokesperson argued that effective ______ were simply not available.
   (A) inconsequential...substitutes
   (B) unusual...alternatives

(C) increasing...procedures
(D) indeterminable...safeguards
(E) proven...antidotes

5. In pollen dating, geologic happenings are dated in terms of each other, and one can get just so far by matching ______ sequences; but in radiocarbon dating the scale of time is measured in ______ terms of centuries or years.
(A) random...selective
(B) irrelevant...usable
(C) vague...relative
(D) independent...absolute
(E) imaginary...calculable

6. An analysis of the ideas in the novel compels an analysis of the form of the work, particularly when form and content are as ______ as they are in *The House of the Seven Gables*.
(A) symptomatic
(B) delineated
(C) integrated
(D) conspicuous
(E) distinctive

7. Although ordinarily skeptical about the purity of Robinson's motives, in this instance Jenkins did not consider Robinson's generosity to be ______ consideration of personal gain.
(A) lacking in
(B) contrary to
(C) alloyed with
(D) mitigated by
(E) repudiated by

Exercise 68

1. The ______ success of any government depends on its ability to ______ both foreign and domestic policies.
(A) political...implement
(B) military...distribute
(C) social...complete
(D) essential...violate
(E) diplomatic...subsidize

2. Although Jungius detected Galileo's ______ in thinking that the curve assumed by a chain hanging freely between two supports was a parabola, he did not ______ what the true form might be.
(A) wisdom...question
(B) rationale...prove
(C) error...discover
(D) sincerity...conceal
(E) ingenuity...understand

3. It is a great ______ to be able to transfer useful genes with as little extra gene material as possible, because the donor's genome may contain, in addition to desirable genes, many genes with ______ effects.
(A) misfortune...unpredictable
(B) disappointment ...superfluous
(C) convenience...exquisite
(D) accomplishment...profound
(E) advantage...deleterious

4. The combination of ________and ________ in Edmund's speech can be starting, especially when he slyly slips in some juicy vulgarity amid the mellifluous circumlocutions of a gentleman of the old school.
(A) tact...innocence

笔记区

(B) raciness...ribaldry

(C) piousness...modesty

(D) elegance...earthiness

(E) propriety...bashfulness 羞怯的

5. The impact of a recently published collection of essays, written during and about the last presidential campaign, is lessened by its timing; it comes too late to affect us with its ______ and too soon for us to read it out of historical______.

(A) foresight...anxiety

(B) research ...consistency

(C) assuredness...skepticism

(D) immediacy...curiosity

(E) veracity...respect

6. Personnel experts say that attractive benefits alone will not always keep ______ executives from changing jobs for better long-range opportunities, but they think the enticements may deter many executives from accepting ______ offers from other companies.

(A) discontented...preferable

(B) ambitious...routine

(C) unqualified...inferior

(D) experienced...superior

(E) dedicated...advantageous

7. The semantic ______ of ancient documents is not unique; even in our own time, many documents are difficult to decipher.

(A) aspect

(B) pattern

(C) opacity

(D) intention

(E) erudition

Exercise 69

1. Although there are weeks of negotiations ahead, and perhaps setbacks and new surprises, leaders of both parties are ______ that their differences can be resolved.
(A) optimistic
(B) perplexed
(C) apprehensive
(D) incredulous
(E) uncertain

2. Every novel invites us to enter a world that is initially strange; our gradual and selective orientation to its manners______'infants' ______ to their environment.
(A) imitates...welcome
(B) completes ...introduction
(C) resembles ...adjustment
(D) alters ...blindness
(E) reinforces ...resistance

3. The most technologically advanced societies have been responsible for the greatest ______; indeed, savagery seems to be in direct proportion to ______.
(A) wars...viciousness
(B) catastrophes...ill-will
(C) atrocities...development
(D) inventions...know-how
(E) triumphs...civilization

4. The little-known but rapidly expanding use of computers in mapmaking is technologically similar to the more ______ uses in designing everything from bolts to satellites.
(A) recent
(B) impromptu
(C) publicized

笔记区

(D) ingenuous
(E) secure

5. The brittle fronds of the Boston fern break easily and become brown, so that the overall appearance of the plant is ______ unless the broken fronds are cut off.
(A) admired
(B) overrated
(C) disparaged
(D) blunted
(E) ruined

6. Many welfare reformers would substitute a single, federally financed income support system for the existing ______ of overlapping programs.
(A) paucity
(B) core
(C) functionalism
(D) participation
(E) welter

7. The blueprints for the new automobile were ______ at first glance, but the designer had been basically too conservative to ______ previous standards of beauty.
(A) striking...flout
(B) impractical...ignore
(C) impeccable...dispel
(D) influential ...assess
(E) confusing...incorporate

BCABDCA
CDB

Exercise 70

1. Even though six players had been injured, the coach announced to the assembled reporters that the team would ______ the championship.
   (A) ignore
   (B) win
   (C) overcome
   (D) demand
   (E) refuse

2. To compensate for the substantial decline in the availability of fossil fuels in future years, we will have to provide at least ______ alternative energy source.
   (A) an anticipated
   (B) an official
   (C) an equivalent
   (D) a derivative
   (E) a redundant

3. Perhaps______, since an ability to communicate effectively is an important trait of any great leader, it has been the ______ Presidents who have delivered the most notable inaugural addresses.
   (A) predictably...exceptional
   (B) invariable...famous
   (C) undeniably...indomitable
   (D) reciprocally...traditionalist
   (E) impractically...influential

4. Postmodern architecture is not concerned with the easy goal of returning to the past but with the more ______ and difficult aim of ______ historical forms into a new and complex whole.
   (A) important...changing
   (B) subtle...integrating

笔 记 区

(C) intellectual...updating
(D) rewarding ...dramatizing
(E) ornamental...compressing

5. Most people are shameless ______ where the very rich are concerned, ______ curious about how they get their money and how they spend it.
(A) prigs...secretly
(B) critics...endlessly
(C) voyeurs...insatiably
(D) exhibitionists...blatantly
(E) ingrates...selfishly

6. Rousseau's short discourse, a work that was generally ______ the cautious, unadorned prose of the day, deviated from that prose style in its ______ discussion of the physical sciences.
(A) critical of ...lengthy
(B) superior to ...austere
(C) bolder than ...intelligent
(D) consistent with ...unrestrained
(E) influenced by ...uninspired

7. Although ______ in her own responses to the plays she reviewed, the theatre critic was, paradoxically, ______ those who would deny that a reviewer must have a single method of interpretation.
(A) dogmatic...impatient with
(B) eclectic...suspicious of
(C) partisan...hostile toward
(D) capricious...intrigued by
(E) indulgent...indebted by

Exercise 71

1. Our young people, whose ______ sensitivities have not yet become ______, have a purer and more immediate response than we do to our environment.
(A) native...excited
(B) keen...calloused
(C) dull...numbed
(D) impartial...objective
(E) sophisticated...perceptive

2. Although Ms. Brown found some of her duties to be ______, her supervision of forty workers was a considerable responsibility.
(A) ambiguous
(B) provisional
(C) menial
(D) unique
(E) mediocre

3. Although it is unusual to denounce museum-goers for not painting, it is quite common, even for those, who are unenthusiastic about sports, to criticize______ for athletic______.
(A) artists...ignorance
(B) spectators...inactivity
(C) athletes...snobbery
(D) scholars...apathy
(E) commentators...partiality

4. The constitutional guarantee or tree speech may have been aimed at protecting native speakers of English from censorship, but it is not a great ______ to interpret it as protecting the right to express oneself in any natural language or dialect.
(A) enigma
(B) extension

(C) sacrifice
(D) condemnation
(E) attenuation

5. Because time in India is conceived statically rather than dynamically, Indian languages emphasize nouns rather than verbs, since nouns express the more ______ aspects of a thing.
(A) paradoxical
(B) prevalent
(C) temporal
(D) successive
(E) stable

6. The ______ of her career was her achievement of her greatest intellectual authority at the very moment when she was ______ of a compelling subject.
(A) irony...assured
(B) dilemma...certain
(C) enigma...cognizant
(D) paradox...bereft
(E) epitome...despairing

7. Ultimately, the book's credibility is strained; the slender, though far from ______, web of evidence presented on one salient point is expected to support a vast ______ of implications.
(A) unconvincing...cacophony
(B) nonexistent...superstructure
(C) indispensable...array
(D) intricate...network
(E) imposing...compendium

Exercise 72

1. When an oppressed group revolts against a society, one must look for the ______ forces that led to the group's ______ that society.
   (A) disparate ...acknowledgment of
   (B) specific ...dependence on
   (C) altered ...redistribution within
   (D) focused ...interference with
   (E) underlying ...alienation from

2. Although his outnumbered troops fought bravely, the general felt he had no choice but to ______ defeat and ______ a retreat.
   (A) hasten...suggest
   (B) seek...try
   (C) oversee...reject
   (D) overcome...request
   (E) acknowledge...order

3. Ambrose Blerce's biographers agree that the Civil War was the central experience of his life, the event to which be constantly returned and the ______ that brought some ______ to the hitherto random pattern of his youth.
   (A) ordeal...coherence
   (B) interruption...continuity
   (C) climax...confusion
   (D) escape...diversion
   (E) hiatus...rigidity

4. Her remarkable______, which first became apparent when she repeatedly defeated the older children at school, eventually earned for her some______ rewards, including a full athletic scholarship and several first-place trophies.
   (A) sportsmanship...academic
   (B) agility...monetary

笔 记 区

(C) modesty...unanticipated

(D) speed...tangible

(E) patience...well-deserved

5. Amid the collapsing or out-of-control mechanical devices, the belching volcano had a disturbingly______ quality, like a character who has stumbled onstage by mistake.

(A) anomalous

(B) overwrought

(C) obdurate

(D) ephemeral

(E) derelict

6. It is an error to regard the imagination as a mainly ______ force; if it destroys and alters, it also______ hitherto isolated beliefs, insights, and mental habits into strongly unified systems.

(A) visionary...conjures

(B) beneficial...converts

(C) revolutionary...fuses

(D) negative...shunts

(E) synthetic...integrates

7. The Neoplatonists' conception of a deity, in which perfection was measured by abundant fecundity, was contradicted by that of the Aristotelians, in which perfection was displayed in the ______ of creation.

(A) profusion

(B) precision

(C) variety

(D) clarity

(E) economy

Exercise 73

1. Stress is experienced when an individual feels that the ______ of the environment ______ that individual's resources for handling them.
   (A) circumstances...intensify
   (B) details...exclude
   (C) demands...exceed
   (D) facets...imply
   (E) benefits...reveal

2. One reason why pertinent fossils are ______ is that crucial stages of evolution occurred in the tropics where it is difficult to explore for fossils, and so their discovery has ______.
   (A) unique....resulted
   (B) unconcealable...declined
   (C) uncommon...lagged
   (D) recent...resumed
   (E) prominent ...failed

3. Superficial differences between the special problems and techniques of the physical sciences and those of the biological sciences are some times cited as evidence for the ______ of biology and for the claim that the methods of physics are therefore not adequate to biological inquiry.
   (A) autonomy
   (B) vitalism
   (C) purposiveness
   (D) obsolescence
   (E) irrelevance

4. For those Puritans who believed that ______ obligations were imposed by divine will, the correct course of action was not withdrawal from the world but conscientious ______ of the duties of business.

(A) practical...mystification
(B) inherent...manipulation
(C) secular...discharge
(D) earthly...disavowal
(E) trying...moderation

5. This new government is faced not only with ______ its economy but also with implementing new rural development programs to ______ the flow of farm workers to the city.
(A) managing...stem 茎、干
(B) offsetting...harness
(C) bolstering...transmit 支撑 加固
(D) challenging...measure
(E) modernizing...subsidize

6. Every new theory not only must ______ the valid predictions of the old theory, but must also explain why those predictions ______ within the range of that old theory.
(A) organize...failed
(B) generate...faltered
(C) promote...functioned
(D) refute...evolved
(E) accommodate...succeeded

7. That the Third Battalion's fifty-percent casualty rate transformed its assault on Hill 306 from a brilliant stratagem into a debacle does not ______ eyewitness reports of its commander's extra-ordinary ______ in deploying his forces.
(A) justify...rapidity
(B) gainsay...cleverness
(C) corroborate...determination
(D) invalidate...brutality
(E) underscore...ineptitude

Exercise 74

1. It is true that the seeds of some plants have ______ after two hundred years of dormancy, but reports that viable seeds have been found in ancient tombs such as the pyramids are entirely______
(A) revived...empirical 以观察或实验为依据的
(B) germinated...unfounded
(C) endured...irrelevant
(D) erupted...reasonable
(E) proliferated...substantiated

2. Both television commercials and programs present ______ view of the material world, one which promotes a standard of living that most of us can probably not attain.
(A) an unrealistic
(B) an imprudent
(C) a standardized
(D) a perplexing
(E) a banal

3. He never ______ the wisdom I had claimed for him, and my friends quickly dismissed my estimate of his ability as ______.
(A) repudiated...irony
(B) inhibited ...propaganda
(C) demonstrated...hyperbole
(D) masked...exaggeration
(E) vindicated...understatement

4. As the creation of new knowledge through science has become ______ resistance to innovation has become less ______ taking the form of inertia rather than direct attack.
(A) controversial ...sporadic

笔 记 区

(B) institutionalized ...aggressive

(C) essential ...effective

(D) public ...circumspect

(E) suspect ...lively

5. Although Darwinism was a profoundly ______ world view, it was essentially passive, since it prescribed no steps to be taken, no victories over nature to be celebrated, no program of triumphs of be successively gained.

(A) limited

(B) repressive

(C) debatable

(D) innovative

(E) paradoxical

6. Plants store a ______ of water in their leaves, stems, or understock to provide themselves with a form of ______ that will carry them through the inevitable drought they must suffer in the wild.

(A) supply...tolerance

(B) hoard...insurance

(C) reservoir...accommodation

(D) provision...restoration

(E) contribution...support

7. The simplicity of the theory—its main attraction—is also its ______ for only by ______the assumptions of the theory is it possible to explain the most recent observations made by researchers.

(A) liability...accepting

(B) virtue...qualifying

(C) downfall...considering

(D) glory...rejecting

(E) undoing...supplementing

解开.打开

Exercise 75

1. Faraday does not ______ any particular theory; she believes that each theory increases our understanding of some dreams but that no single theory can ______ them all.
   (A) endorse...explain
   (B) discuss...simplify
   (C) mention...replace
   (D) evaluate...identify
   (E) criticize...eradicate

2. The losing animal in a struggle saves itself from destruction by an act of ______, an act usually recognized and ______ by the winner.
   (A) submission...accepted
   (B) hostility...avoided
   (C) bluffing ...reaffirmed
   (D) anger...condoned
   (E) hatred...duplicated

3. Since the process of atherosclerosis cannot be _______ in humans, the best treatment known at this time is ______ of the disease.
   (A) reversed...prevention
   (B) discovered...remission
   (C) defined...explanation
   (D) alleviated...detection
   (E) precipitated...containment

4. The prime minister tried to act but the plans were ______ by her cabinet.
   (A) frustrated
   (B) discussed
   (C) embellished
   (D) overlooked

笔 记 区

(E) unleashed

5. An example of an illegitimate method of argument is to lump______cases together deliberately under the ______ that the same principles apply to each.

(A) unsuitable...impression

(B) disputable...stipulation

(C) irrelevant...assumption

(D) dissimilar...pretense

(E) indeterminate...rationale

6. The essence of belief is the establishment of ______; different beliefs are distinguishable by the different modes of action to which they give rise.

(A) love

(B) practice 练习、实践

(C) trust

(D) commitments

(E) allegiances 拥护、忠诚

7. The concept of timelessness is paradoxical from the start ,for adult consciousness is ______ by the awareness of duration.

(A) intrigued

(B) repelled

(C) measured

(D) accelerated

(E) permeated

笔 记 区

AECDEAA
AD

Exercise 76

1. There are simply no ______ for buying stock in certain industries since rapidly changing environmental restrictions will make a profitable return on any investment very unlikely.
(A) incentives
(B) arrangements
(C) explanations
(D) conditions
(E) procedures

拒绝、断绝关系

2. The repudiation of Puritanism in seventeenth-century England expressed itself not only in retaliatory laws to ______ Puritans, but also in a general attitude of ______ for Puritans.
(A) restrict...contempt
(B) regulate...regard
(C) benefit...affection
(D) repress...respect
(E) evade...hatred

回避

3. The harmonious accommodation reached by the warring factions exemplifies the axiom that ______ is possible among people of goodwill, even when they have previously held quite ______ perspectives.
(A) candor...indistinguishable
(B) tension...congenial
(C) agreement...unequivocal 清楚明白的
(D) compromise...antagonistic
(E) coexistence...fixed

4. Because the order in which the parts of speech appear in the sentences of a given language is decided merely by custom, it is______ to maintain that every departure from that order constitutes a ______of a natural law.

笔 记 区

(A) traditional...transformation
(B) conventional...transgression
(C) necessary...prototype
(D) unjustifiable...violation
(E) unreasonable...formulation

5. Many philosophers agree that the verbal aggression of profanity in certain radical newspapers is not ______ or childish, but an assault on ______ essential to the revolutionaries purpose.
(A) belligerent...fallibility
(B) serious...propriety
(C) insolent...sociability
(D) deliberate...affectation
(E) trivial...decorum

6. There is no necessary intrinsic connection between a word and the thing it refers to, the relationship is purely ______.
(A) conventional
(B) consistent
(C) strategic
(D) illustrative
(E) problematical

7. Because the report contained much more information than the reviewers needed to see,the author was asked to submit a ______ instead.
(A) compendium
(B) soliloquy 自言自语
(C) treatise
(D) prerequisite
(E) critique

笔 记 区

GRE 填空答案

Exercise 1	CDEECBD
Exercise 2	ACCCDBC
Exercise 3	EEEDBBB
Exercise 4	EDDEEED
Exercise 5	AABECCE
Exercise 6	AEADDDC
Exercise 7	AEDBADC
Exercise 8	BBBEBDE
Exercise 9	CDBBDAB
Exercise 10	CAEEBBE
Exercise 11	DCDCADA
Exercise 12	BDBCEEB
Exercise 13	EBDCEDB
Exercise 14	EBECCEE
Exercise 15	CABDCEE
Exercise 16	DDCCDBE
Exercise 17	EEAECCB
Exercise 18	AADEECE
Exercise 19	CAABBEB
Exercise 20	CDADCCC
Exercise 21	CCECBBD
Exercise 22	BAAAECC
Exercise 23	ADDEBAE
Exercise 24	ACBADBC
Exercise 25	BCACEED
Exercise 26	DAAAECA
Exercise 27	CBDACDB
Exercise 28	DEAEACD
Exercise 29	CBBEDDC
Exercise 30	CCDBEBB
Exercise 31	BBBBAEA
Exercise 32	AECEECE
Exercise 33	EBBCCAC
Exercise 34	DDBACBA
Exercise 35	ACDBAED
Exercise 36	DEBDECB
Exercise 37	CDBDBBA
Exercise 38	BCDDBCE
Exercise 39	EDEABBD
Exercise 40	ACCCCDD
Exercise 41	CABABAB
Exercise 42	CBADCCE
Exercise 43	CABBDEE
Exercise 44	ABCBACE
Exercise 45	AAACCDB
Exercise 46	BCEECAD
Exercise 47	DCBDBBC
Exercise 48	BDAAADE
Exercise 49	BEECDED
Exercise 50	CDAADDE
Exercise 51	DEDBDAD
Exercise 52	DECCEAE
Exercise 53	AEBEBEE
Exercise 54	CDBCEDD
Exercise 55	CACBEBE
Exercise 56	BEBCCDB
Exercise 57	CECBCDC
Exercise 58	EDABBEC
Exercise 59	CEBEADC
Exercise 60	BAEAEBE

Exercise 61	ECBDCEE	Exercise 69	ACCCEEA
Exercise 62	BDDBDDB	Exercise 70	BCABCDB
Exercise 63	CEEACCA	Exercise 71	BCBBEDB
Exercise 64	BEBCDAB	Exercise 72	EEADACE
Exercise 65	CBEDCDB	Exercise 73	CCACAEB
Exercise 66	CEDDDDD	Exercise 74	BACBDBE
Exercise 67	CDBADCC	Exercise 75	AAAADBE
Exercise 68	ACEDDBC	Exercise 76	AADDEAA

笔 记 区

GRE 补充填空题

1. "The show must go on" is the oldest ________ of show business; every true performer lives by that creed.
   (A) euphemism
   (B) allegory
   (C) precursor
   (D) tenet
   (E) corroboration

2. ________ James Baldwin, who wrote of black Americans as being in a perpetual state of rage, Mr. Cose remarks that few human beings could ________ the psychic toll of uninterrupted anger.
   (A) Corroborating...endure
   (B) Refuting...enhance
   (C) Dismissing...refine
   (D) Challenging...survive
   (E) Upholding...weather

3. ________ by life's ________ , the last emperor of China worked as a lowly gardener in the palace over which he had once ruled.
   (A) Fortified...generosity
   (B) Deluded...coincidences
   (C) Humbled...vicissitudes
   (D) Venerated...survivors
   (E) Recognized...impostors

4. ________ his broker had told him that the stock was a investment, he insisted on buying 100 shares.
   (A) Because...speculative
   (B) Although...precarious
   (C) Since...negligible
   (D) Although...formidable
   (E) Because...dwindling

5. A ________ glance pays ________ attention to details.
   (A) furtive...meticulous
   (B) cursory...little

(C) cryptic...close
(D) keen...scanty
(E) fleeting...vigilant

6. A ________ person is one who will ________ something on the slightest of evidence.
(A) restive...forget
(B) garrulous...criticize
(C) maudlin...censure
(D) phlegmatic...condemn
(E) credulous...believe

7. A New World lizard, the basilisk, occasionally does something that seems to ________ physics: it runs across the surface of water for distances of up to thirty feet.
(A) defy
(B) quantify
(C) assess
(D) exemplify
(E) corroborate

8. A born teller of tales, Olsen used her impressive ________ skills to advantage in her story "I Stand Here Ironing."
(A) domestic
(B) metaphysical
(C) narrative
(D) diagnostic
(E) argumentative

9. A code of ethics governing the behavior of physicians during epidemics did not exist until 1846 when it was ________ by the American Medical Association.
(A) rescinded
(B) promulgated
(C) presupposed
(D) depreciated
(E) implied

10. A diligent scholar, she devoted herself ________ to the completion of the book.
(A) assiduously
(B) ingenuously
(C) theoretically
(D) voluminously
(E) sporadically

11. A hypothesis must not only account for what we already know, but it must also be ________ by continued observation.
(A) refuted
(B) interrupted
(C) verified
(D) discredited

(E) outmoded

12. A journalist rather than a scholar, Mr. Cose seems nevertheless to be ________ most of the serious studies relevant to his topic.
(A) overawed by
(B) ignorant of
(C) associated with
(D) wearied by
(E) familiar with

13. A leading philosopher of our time, Ludwig Wittgenstein, laid down a ________ to which good historians ________ : "Of that of which nothing is known nothing can be said. "
(A) burden...protest
(B) law...amend
(C) rule...adhere
(D) maxim...succumb
(E) weapon...surrender

14. A major outbreak of food poisoning in 1993 underlined the serious ________ in the then-current system of food inspection.
(A) expectations
(B) innovations
(C) objectivity
(D) deficiencies
(E) uniformity

15. A man incapable of ________ action, he never had an opinion about something that he had not worked up beforehand, fashioning it with lengthy care.
(A) premeditated
(B) coherent
(C) spontaneous
(D) calculated
(E) self-conscious

16. A sense of fairness ________ that the punishment should fit the crime; yet, in actual practice, judicial decisions ________ greatly for the same type of criminal offense.
(A) assumes...coincide
(B) relegates...deviate
(C) accumulates...simplify
(D) insists...compromise
(E) dictates...vary

17. A subway modernization program intended to ________ a host of problems ranging from dangerous tracks to overcrowded stairwells has failed to meet its schedule for repairs.
(A) augment
(B) initiate
(C) deplore
(D) disclose

笔 记 区

(E) eliminate

18. Abandoning the moral principles of his youth, the aging emperor Tiberius led a ________ , wanton life.
(A) celibate
(B) rudimentary
(C) debauched
(D) circumspect
(E) peripatetic

19. According to Lionel Trilling, the paradox of liberalism was that in its quest for freedom it must move toward greater organization, stricter legislation, and increasing ________ .
(A) anarchy
(B) self-realization
(C) stagnation
(D) control
(E) levity

20. According to a noted art critic, one would have to be completely immune to the sensuous pleasures of painting to be ________ Lucien Freud's mesmerizing art.
(A) drawn to
(B) overcome by
(C) enamored of
(D) unaffected by
(E) consistent about

21. According to poet John Berryman, there were so many ways to ________ a poem that it was quite amazing good ones ever gotwritten.
(A) dedicate
(B) begin
(C) ruin
(D) recite
(E) categorize

22. According to the Senator, it was not ________ for a politician in search of votes to ________ a mother on the beauty of her plain child; it was merely sound political common sense.
(A) kindness...ridicule
(B) folly...intimidate
(C) hypocrisy...compliment
(D) sensitivity...evaluate
(E) wisdom...reprimand

23. Achaeologists are involved in ________ Mayan temples in Central America, uncovering the old ruins in order to learn more about the civilization they represent.
(A) demolishing
(B) incapacitating
(C) excavating
(D) worshiping
(E) adapting

笔 记 区

24. Actors fade out of view with depressing frequency; the theater is a ________ profession at best.
(A) romantic
(B) demanding
(C) chancy
(D) disinterested
(E) degenerate

25. Advances in health care have lengthened life spans, lowered infant mortality rates, and, thus, ________ the overpopulation problem.
(A) eliminated
(B) aggravated
(C) minimized
(D) distorted
(E) discouraged

26. Afraid that the ________ nature of the plays being presented would corrupt the morals of their audiences, the Puritans closed the theaters in 1642.
(A) mediocre
(B) fantastic
(C) profound
(D) lewd
(E) witty

27. After reading numbers of biographies recounting dysfunctions and disasters, failed marriages and failed careers, Joyce Carol Oates ________ a word to ________ the genre:pathography, the story of diseased lives.
(A) invented......curtail
(B) reiterated...criticize
(C) hypothesized...indict
(D) dismissed...obscure
(E) coined...describe

28. After the lonely rigors of writing, Mr. Doyle enjoys the ________ aspects of filmmaking.
(A) impersonal
(B) transitory
(C) narrative
(D) social
(E) profitable

29. Aimed at curbing European attempts to seize territory in the Americas, the Monroe Doctrine was a warning to ________ foreign powers.
(A) magnanimous
(B) credulous
(C) reticent
(D) predatory
(E) allied

30. All critics have agreed that the opera's score is ________ , but, curiously, no two critics haye

笔 记 区

agreed which passages to praise and which to damn.

(A) intolerable

(B) melodious

(C) unsurpassed

(D) conventional

(E) uneven

31. Although Barbara Tuchman never earned a graduate degree, she nonetheless ________ a scholarly career as a historian noted for her vivid style and ________ erudition.

(A) interrupted...deficient

(B) relinquished...immense

(C) abandoned...capricious

(D) pursued...prodigious

(E) followed...scanty

32. Although Britain's film makers often produce fine films, they are studiously ________ and rarely aim at a mass market.

(A) commercial

(B) viable

(C) derivative

(D) elitist

(E) collaborative

33. Although Henry was not in general a sentimental man, occasionally he would feel a touch of ________ for the old days and would contemplate making a brief excursion to Boston to revisit his childhood friends.

(A) exasperation

(B) chagrin

(C) nostalgia

(D) lethargy

(E) anxiety

34. Although I have always been confused by our ________ system, I ________ traveling on the subways occasionally.

(A) mercantile...remember

(B) monetary...deplore

(C) social...ponder

(D) transit...relish

(E) revolutionary...prefer

35. Although Josephine Tey is arguably as good a mystery writer as Agatha Christie, she is clearly far less ________ than Christie, having written only six books in comparison to Christie¡äs sixty.

(A) coherent

(B) prolific

(C) equivocal

(D) pretentious

(E) gripping

36. Although Roman original contributions to government, jurisprudence, and engineering are commonly acknowledged, the artistic legacy of the Roman world continues to be judged widely as ________ the magnificent Greek traditions that preceded it.

(A) an improvement on

(B) an echo of

(C) a resolution of

(D) a precursor of

(E) a consummation of

37. Although a few of her contemporaries ________ her book, most either ignored it or mocked it.

(A) dismissed

(B) disregarded

(C) deprecated

(D) misconstrued

(E) appreciated

38. Although gregarious by nature, Lisa became quiet and ________ after she was unexpectedly laid off from work.

(A) autonomous

(B) susceptible

(C) assertive

(D) withdrawn

(E) composed

39. Although he generally observed the adage "Look before you leap," in this instance he was ________ acting in an unconsidered fashion.

(A) chary of

(B) impervious to

(C) precipitate in

(D) hesitant about

(E) conventional in

40. Although he had spent many hours at the computer trying to solve the problem, he was the first to admit that the final solution was ________ and not the ________ of his labor.

(A) trivial...cause

(B) incomplete...intent

(C) adequate...concern

(D) schematic...fault

(E) fortuitous...result

41. Although he had the numerous films to his credit and a reputation for technical ________ , the moviemaker lacked originality; all his films were sadly ________ of the work of others.

(A) skill...independent

(B) ability...unconscious

(C) expertise...derivative

(D) competence...contradictory

(E) blunders...enamored

笔 记 区

42. Although he is ________ about the problems that still confront blacks in ballet, Mitchell nevertheless is optimistic about the future, especially that of his own dance company.
(A) hopeful
(B) uninformed
(C) abstract
(D) realistic
(E) unconcerned

43. Although he was widely celebrated as a radio and motion picture star in the 1940s, George Burns enjoyed his greatest ________ after his return to the screen in the "Oh God" films of the 1930s.
(A) respite
(B) collaboration
(C) renown
(D) disappointment
(E) inducement

44. Although in his seventies at the time of the interview, Picasso proved alert and insightful, his faculties ________ despite the inevitable toll of the years.
(A) atrophied
(B) diminished
(C) intact
(D) useless
(E) impaired

45. Although most worthwhile criticism concentrates on the positive, one should not ________ praise everything.
(A) argumentatively
(B) constructively
(C) derogatorily
(D) analytically
(E) indiscriminately

46. Although newscasters often use the terms Chicano and Latino ________ , students of Hispanic-American culture are profoundly aware of the ________ the two.
(A) interchangeably...dissimilarities between
(B) indifferently...equivalence of
(C) deprecatingly...controversies about
(D) unerringly...significance of
(E) confidently...origins of

47. Although similar to mice in many physical characteristics, voles may be ________ mice by the shortness oft heir tails.
(A) distinguished from
(B) classified with
(C) related to
(D) categorized as
(E) enumerated with

笔 记 区

48. Although the death of his dog had saddened him markedly, his computer designing skills remained completely ________

(A) twisted

(B) unaffected

(C) incapable

(D) repaired

(E) demolished

49. Although, as wife of President John Adams, Abigail Adams sought a greater voice for women, she was not a feminist in the modern sense; she ________ the ________ view of women as "beings placed by providence"under male protection.

(A) anticipated...current

(B) regretted...heretical

(C) distorted...outmoded

(D) repudiated...radical

(E) accepted...traditional

50. Always less secure in herself than she liked to make out, she too often disagreement as ________ and opposition as treachery.

(A) rewarded...virtue

(B) construed...betrayal

(C) condemned...detachment

(D) invited...provocation

(E) interpreted...drollery

51. Always trying to look on the bright side of every situation, she is a born ________ .

(A) opportunist

(B) antagonist

(C) optimist

(D) maverick

(E) zealot

52. American culture now stigmatizes, and sometimes even heavily ________ . behavior that was once taken for granted: overt racism, cigarette smoking, the use of sexual stereotypes.

(A) advocates

(B) penalizes

(C) ignores

(D) indoctrinates

(E) advertises

53. Americans have always been rightfully ________ unnecessary government coercion, feeling that the government should use its powers sparingly.

(A) disarmed by

(B) chary about

(C) dependent on

(D) amenable to

(E) enthusiastic about

笔 记 区

54. An experienced politician who knew better than to launch a campaign in troubled political waters, she intended to wait for a more ________ occasion before she announced her plans.
(A) propitious
(B) provocative
(C) unseemly
(D) questionable
(E) theoretical

55. An optimistic supporter of the women¡äs movement, Kubota contends that recent ________ by Japanese women in the business word are meaningful and indicative of ________ opportunity to come.
(A) advances...diminished
(B) strides...greater
(C) innovations...marginal
(D) retreats...theoretical
(E) failures...hidden

56. An unattractive feature of this memoir is the casually dismissive, often downright ________ , comments the author makes about almost all of her former colleagues.
(A) elegiac
(B) euphemistic
(C) objective
(D) contemptuous
(E) laudatory

57. Anthropologists traditionally argue that the male-female division of labor in huntergatherer societies arose because it ________ the nuclear family's joint interests and thereby represented a sound, ________ strategy.
(A) impaired...collaborative
(B) respected...divisive
(C) ignored...disinterested
(D) restricted...provisional
(E) promoted...cooperative

58. Are we to turn into spineless ________ , afraid to take a ________ stand, unable to answer a question without pussyfooting?
(A) disciples...positive
(B) hedonists...compromising
(C) criminals...defiant
(D) critics...constructive
(E) equivocators...forthright

59. As Reginald Machell's lavishly carved throne clearly illustrates, California craftsmen were not afraid of ________ .
(A) competition
(B) embellishment
(C) imitation
(D) expediency

笔 记 区

(E) antiquity

60. As a product of the Soviet literary establishment, the author was brave enough to ________ the hand that fed him, but not heroic enough to bite it.
(A) give up
(B) nibble at
(C) cringe from
(D) worship
(E) devour

61. As a scientific document, the book should stand for several years until further ________ again make revision ________ .
(A) developments...impossible
(B) obstacles...optional
(C) attempts...undesirable
(D) failures...detrimental
(E) advances...necessary

62. As a sportscaster, Cosell was apparently never ________ ; he made ________ comments about every boxing match he covered.
(A) excited...hysterical
(B) relevant...pertinent
(C) satisfied...disparaging
(D) amazed...awe-struck
(E) impressed...laudatory

63. As an outstanding publisher, Alfred Knopf was able to make occasional ________ , but his had judgment was tolerated in view of his tremendous ________ .
(A) appearances...energy
(B) mistakes...success
(C) remarks...connections
(D) enemies...audacity
(E) conferences...patience

64. As delicate and ________as insect bodies are, it is remarkable that over the ages enough of them have ________ , preserved in amber, for scientists to trace insect evolution.
(A) beautiful...disappeared
(B) fragile...survived
(C) impervious...multiplied
(D) refined...awakened
(E) indestructible...evolved

65. As ecologists recently ________ in studying the effects of naturally induced forest fires, some phenomena that appear on the surface to be destructive often have a hidden ________ effect on balance.
(A) disproved...beneficial
(B) discovered...positive
(C) hypothesized...catastrophic

笔 记 区

(D) disclosed...unecological
(E) determined...disastrous

66. As former Supreme Court Justice Warren Burger was fond of pointing out, many lawyers are not legal hotshots; they often come to court ________ and ________ professional skills.
(A) ill-prepared...lacking
(B) hot-tempered...criticizing
(C) reluctant...demonstrating
(D) argumentative...manifesting
(E) conservative...excelling

67. As founder and president of the Children¡äs Defense Fund, Marian Wright Edelman has ensured that, even though the young cannot vote or make campaign contributions, they are nevertheless not ________ in Washington.
(A) represented
(B) distrusted
(C) ignored
(D) committed
(E) welcome

68. As matter condenses out of the thin disk of hot gas and dust revolving around a new sun, it ________ into larger particles, just as snowflakes stick together as they fall.
(A) crashes
(B) protrudes
(C) coalesces
(D) evaporates
(E) dissolves

69. As more people try to navigate the legal system by themselves, representing themselves in court and drawing up their own wills and contracts, the question arises whether they will be able to ________ judicial ________ without lawyers to guide them.
(A) await...decisions
(B) overturn...stipulations
(C) avoid...quagmires
(D) forfeit...penalties
(E) arouse...enmity

70. As news of his indictment spread through the town, the citizens began to ________ him and to avoid meeting him.
(A) ostracize
(B) congratulate
(C) desecrate
(D) minimize
(E) harass

71. As surprising as the new findings are, Dr. Wilson said he would not characterize them as ________.
(A) sound
(B) revolutionary
(C) equitable

笔记区

(D) evident
(E) abstruse

72. At a time when biographies that debunk their subjects are all the rage, it is refreshing to have one idol who not only lives up to her legend but ________ it.
(A) complicates
(B) surpasses
(C) compromises
(D) rejects
(E) subverts

73. At first ________ were simply that:straightforward firsthand testimonials about the ________ of a product.
(A) trademarks...contents
(B) creeds...excellence
(C) prejudices...flaws
(D) reprimands...benefits
(E) endorsements...virtues

74. At the height of the storm, the savages tried to ________ the angry gods by offering sacrifices.
(A) modify
(B) appall
(C) vilify
(D) propitiate
(E) instigate

75. At the present time, we are suffering from ________ of stories about the war; try writing about another subject.
(A) a calumny
(B) a dearth
(C) an insurgence
(D) a plethora
(E) an inhibition

76. Because auto repair places have such ________ rates, many community colleges have ________ courses in automotive mechanics.
(A) shattering...planned
(B) exorbitant...instituted
(C) impertinent...discussed
(D) reasonable...introduced
(E) intolerable...discontinued

77. Because fruit juice fills babies' small stomachs and ruins their appetite for foods that contain nutrients they ________ , consuming large quantities can actually prove ________ to babies less than 24 months old.
(A) prefer...beneficial
(B) choose...counterproductive
(C) require...helpful

(D) need...detrimental

(E) ingest...advantageous

78. Because he had abandoned his post and joined forces with the Indians, his fellow officers considered the hero of Dances with Wolves a ________ .

(A) martinet

(B) braggart

(C) renegade

(D) skinflint

(E) laggard

79. Because he had assumed that the child's first, fierce rush of grief would quickly ________ , Murdstone was astonished to find him still ________ .

(A) subside...disconsolate

(B) fade...irresolute

(C) elapse...disingenuous

(D) escalate...forlorn

(E) dwindle...dormant

80. Because he is so ________ , we can never predict what course he will take at any moment.

(A) incoherent

(B) superficial

(C) capricious

(D) deleterious

(E) conventional

81. Because he saw no ________ to the task assigned him, he worked at it in a very ________ way.

(A) function...systematic

(B) method...dutiful

(C) purpose...diligent

(D) end...rigid

(E) point...perfunctory

82. Because he was ________ by nature, he preferred reading a book in the privacy of his own study to visiting a night club with friends.

(A) an exhibitionist

(B) a hedonist

(C) an adversary

(D) an egoist

(E) an introvert

83. Because he was ________ in the performance of his duties, his employers could not ________ his work.

(A) derelict...quarrel over

(B) dilatory...grumble at

(C) undisciplined...object to

(D) assiduous...complain about

(E) mandatory...count on

84. Because he was ________ , he shunned human society.
(A) a misanthrope
(B) an oligarch
(C) an anomaly
(D) a stereotype
(E) a nonentity

85. Because his time was limited, Weng decided to read the ________ novel War and Peace in ________ edition.
(A) wordy...an unedited
(B) lengthy...an abridged
(C) famous...a modem
(D) romantic...an autographed
(E) popular...a complete

86. Because it had not been blasted into a stable orbit, the satellite moved ________ through space.
(A) innocuously
(B) gradually
(C) erratically
(D) effortlessly
(E) routinely

87. Because it was already known that retroviruses could cause cancer in animals, it seemed only ________ to search for similar cancer-causing viruses in human beings.
(A) culpable
(B) charitable
(C) hypothetical
(D) logical
(E) negligent

88. Because of his ________ driving, the other car was forced to turn off the road or be hit.
(A) perceptive
(B) negligent
(C) resourceful
(D) placid
(E) exemplary

89. Because of its inclination to ________ , most Indian art is ________ Japanese art, where symbols have been minimized and meaning has been conveyed by the merest suggestion.
(A) exaggerate...related to
(B) imitate...superior to
(C) understate...reminiscent of
(D) overdraw...similar to
(E) sentimentalize...supportive of

90. Because of its strength and adhesiveness, ________ qualities in nest building, many species of birds incorporate silk into their nests.
(A) questionable

笔 记 区

(B) intangible
(C) invaluable
(D) hypothetical
(E) irrelevant

91. Because of the trauma they have experienced, survivors of a major catastrophe are likely to exhibit ________ of behavior and may require the aid of competent therapists.
(A) concessions
(B) diminutions
(C) aberrations
(D) restrictions
(E) altercations

92. Because of their frequent disarray, confusion, and loss of memory , those hit by lightning while alone are sometimes ________ victims of assault.
(A) mistaken for
(B) attracted to
(C) unaware of
(D) avoided by
(E) useful to

93. Because our supply of fossil fuel has been sadly ________ , we must find ________ sources of energy.
(A) stored...hoarded
(B) compensated...significant
(C) exhausted...inefficient
(D) increased...available
(E) depleted...alternate

94. Because the apelike members of Australopithecus afarensis were capable both of walking and of swinging through trees, the anthropologist described them as a mosaic, bipedal from the waist down and ________ from the waist up.
(A) ethereal
(B) arboreal
(C) dysfunctional
(D) articulated
(E) pedestrian

95. Because the damage to his car had been ________ , Michael decided he wouldn't bother to report the matter to his insurance company.
(A) intermittent
(B) gratuitous
(C) negligible
(D) spontaneous
(E) significant

96. Because the majority of the evening cable TV programs available dealt with violence and sex, the parents decided that the programs were ________ for the children to watch.

笔 记 区

(A) exclusive
(B) acceptable
(C) instructive
(D) inappropriate
(E) unnecessary

97. Because vast organizations are an inevitable element in modern life, it is ________ to aim at their abolition.
(A) necessary
(B) important
(C) customary
(D) realistic
(E) futile

98. Because we have completed our analysis of the major components of the proposed project, we are free to devote the remainder of this session to a study of the project's ________ details.
(A) lurid
(B) scrupulous
(C) unquestionable
(D) incidental
(E) involuntary

99. Before the inflation ________ , one could have had a complete meal in a restaurant for a dollar, including the tip, whereas today a hot dog, coffee, and dessert would ________ add up to two or three times that much.
(A) spiral...indubitably
(B) cancellation rapidly
(C) problem...improbably
(D) abundance...consequently
(E) incidence...radically

100. Being cynical, he was reluctant to ________ the ________ of any kind act until he had ruled out all possible secret, uncharitable motives.
(A) question...benevolence
(B) acknowledge...wisdom
(C) credit...unselfishness
(D) endure...loss
(E) witness...outcome

101. Biographer Janet Malcolm maintains that biography is a spurious art, for the orderly narrative it creates is ________ ; the "facts"aren't facts at all, but literary ________ .
(A) illusory...inventions
(B) genuine...commonplaces
(C) informative...allusions
(D) brilliant...triumphs
(E) sincere...criticisms

102. Biography is a literary genre whose primary ________ is an ability to ________imaginatively

笔 记 区

the inner life of a subject on the basis of all the knowable external evidence.

(A) requisite...reconstruct

(B) consequence...disregard

(C) peculiarity...envision

(D) weapon...undermine

(E) claim...counteract

103. Biologists categorize many of the world's environments as deserts: regions where the ________ availability of some key factor, such as water, sunlight, or an essential nutrient, places sharp constraints on the existence of living things.

(A) ready

(B) gradual

(C) limited

(D) nearby

(E) unprecedented

104. Black religion was in part a protest movement—a protest against a system and a society that was ________ designed to ________the dignity of a segment of God's creation.

(A) unintentionally...reflect

(B) explicitly...foster

(C) inevitably...assess

(D) deliberately...demean

(E) provocatively...enhance

105. Boccherini was a good and interesting composer whose reputation has no sufficiently ________ the decline into which it fell after his death.

(A) contributed to

(B) benefited from

(C) recovered from

(D) conflicted with

(E) derived from

106. Breaking with established musical conventions, Stravinsky was ________ composer whose heterodox works infuriated the traditionalists of his day.

(A) a derivative

(B) an iconoclastic

(C) an uncontroversial

(D) a venerated

(E) a trite

107. British ________ contemporary art has been an obstacle even for modem artists now revered as great, such as Francis Bacon and Lucian Freud, who were ________ for years before winning acceptance.

(A) veneration of...eulogized

(B) indifference to...dismissed

(C) disdain for...lauded

(D) ignorance of...studied

(E) intolerance of...vindicated

笔 记 区

108. British collectors are notorious for their ________ of interest in ________ art, much preferring to collect antiques and "important"pictures by long-dead artists.
(A) wealth...modem
(B) growth...abstract
(C) lack...posthumous
(D) resurgence...innovative
(E) dearth...contemporary

109. Burdened by debt, Lydgate abandons his dreams of reforming medicine to take a conventional but ________ practice in London.
(A) lucrative
(B) ordinary
(C) innovative
(D) intangible
(E) exotic

110. By communicating through pointing and making gestures, Charles was able to overcome any ________ difficulties that arose during his recent trip to Japan.
(A) peripatetic
(B) linguistic
(C) plausible
(D) monetary
(E) territorial

111. By dint of much practice in the laboratory, the anatomy student became ________ and was able to manipulate her dissecting tools with either hand.
(A) practical
(B) tricky
(C) ambiguous
(D) ambidextrous
(E) ambivalent

112. By nature Toshiro was ________ , given to striking up casual conversations with strangers he encountered at bus stops or check-out stands.
(A) diffident
(B) observant
(C) reticent
(D) gregarious
(E) laconic

113. By putting the entire Woolf archive on microfilm, the project directors hope to make the contents of the manuscripts more ________ to scholars.
(A) accessible
(B) objective
(C) appealing
(D) implicit
(E) relevant

笔 记 区

114. Cancer cells are normal cells run riot, growing and multiplying out of ________ .

(A) spite
(B) danger
(C) control
(D) apathy
(E) range

115. China's economic growth curve after reform resembles an airplane taking off, whereas the former Soviet Union¡äs resembles a submarine ________ .

(A) floating
(B) soaring
(C) maneuvering
(D) descending
(E) veering

116. Compared with the ostentatious glamour of opera, classical song (increasingly called lieder everywhere) is a more ________ tradition.

(A) articulate
(B) unrepresentative
(C) subdued
(D) broad-minded
(E) worldly

117. Complaints about the inanity of popular leisure activities, long a staple of American intellectual life, are routinely ________ these days as nostalgic elitism.

(A) lauded
(B) reinforced
(C) celebrated
(D) offered
(E) dismissed

118. Contemporary critics often ________ the poet Longfellow as a simple sentimentalist who relied too much on poetic meters only suitable for light verse.

(A) heed
(B) endorse
(C) dismiss
(D) embellish
(E) acclaim

119. Contrary to her customary ________ behavior, Susan began leaving parties early to seek the solitude of her room.

(A) reclusive
(B) circumspect
(C) decorous
(D) gregarious
(E) altruistic

笔 记 区

120. Courteously and ________ , but persistently, the members of the special investigatory commission asked question after question of all the President's aides.
(A) intrusively
(B) belligerently
(C) urbanely
(D) remorselessly
(E) intermittently

121. Critics ________ the ________ in developing the new weather satellite to unexpected problems in manufacturing and testing its components.
(A) credit...timeliness
(B) impute...success
(C) attribute...delay
(D) assign...importance
(E) deny...threat

122. Critics of the welfare system argue that, rather than aiding people's efforts to govern their own lives, it ________ their independence.
(A) supports
(B) saps
(C) hastens
(D) renews
(E) abets

123. Crowther maintained that the current revival was the most fatuous and ________ production of the entire theatrical season.
(A) gripping
(B) inane
(C) prophetic
(D) memorable
(E) salubrious

124. Curious____ of Florence's history is that this great center of Italian ________ should time and again have been home to acts of appalling savagery and inhumanity.
(A) example...conflict
(B) paradox...civilization
(C) result...brutality
(D) convention...cultures
(E) distinction...quality

125. Deeply ________ by the insult to his dignity, he maintained that no true gentleman would accept such an calmly.
(A) mortified...opportunity
(B) incensed...affront
(C) puzzled...honor
(D) shamed...iconoclasm
(E) gratified...admonition

笔记区

126. Deloria has his detractors, but his critics have had amazingly ________ success at shaking his self-confidence or ________ his reputation.
(A) great...repairing
(B) widespread...bolstering
(C) little...denting
(D) small...enhancing
(E) poor...restoring

127. Despite all its ________ , a term of enlistment in the Peace Corps can be both stirring and satisfying to a college graduate still undecided on a career.
(A) rewards
(B) renown
(C) adventures
(D) romance
(E) frustrations

128. Despite an affected ________ which convinced casual observers that he was indifferent about his painting and enjoyed only frivolity, Warhol cared deeply about his art and labored at it ________ .
(A) nonchalance...diligently
(B) empathy...methodically
(C) fervor...secretly
(D) gloom...intermittently
(E) hysteria...sporadically

129. Despite careful restoration and cleaning of the murals in the 1960s, the colors slowly but steadily ________ .
(A) persisted
(B) embellished
(C) saturated
(D) deteriorated
(E) stabilized

130. Despite her compassionate nature, the new nominee to the Supreme Court was singleminded and ________ in her strict ________ the letter of the law.
(A) merciful...interpretation of
(B) uncompromising...adherence to
(C) dilatory...affirmation of
(D) vindictive...deviation from
(E) lenient...dismissal of

131. Despite her father's ________ that "a woman¡äs place is in the home" and a ________ reception from her professors and fellow graduate students, Marian Cleeves went on to become the first woman to receive a doctorate in anatomy from the University of California at Berkeley.
(A) warning...gratifying
(B) reprimand...lavish
(C) encouragement...respectful

(D) admonition...cool

(E) maxim...hospitable

132. Despite some personal habits that most people would find repulsive, naked mole rats are ________ housekeepers.

(A) slovenly

(B) indifferent

(C) meticulous

(D) perfunctory

(E) repugnant

133. Despite the ________ discussions of recent months, observers say that the administration and the developer have made progress in their negotiations and are close to ________ on a purchase price.

(A) amicable...haggling

(B) acrimonious...defaulting

(C) heated...agreeing

(D) fruitful...settling

(E) constructive...compromising

134. Despite the ________ of the materials with which he worked, many of Tiffany's glass masterpieces have survived for more than seventy years.

(A) beauty

(B) translucence

(C) abundance

(D) majesty

(E) fragility

135. Despite the___ size of her undergraduate class, the professor made a point of gettingto know as many as possible of the more than 700 students personally.

(A) negligible

(B) modest

(C) infinitesimal

(D) daunting

(E) moderate

136. Despite the current expansion of membership in America, the governing body of world fencing fears that fencing could be in danger of if it does not become more ________ to spectators.

(A) monotony...intelligible

(B) overcrowding...resistant

(C) extinction...accessible

(D) corruption...cordial

(E) remoteness...handy

137. Despite the growing ________ of Hispanic actors in the American theater, many Hispanic experts feel that the Spanishspeaking population is ________ on the stage.

(A) decrease...inappropriate

(B) emergence...visible

笔 记 区

(C) prominence...underrepresented

(D) skill...alienated

(E) number...misdirected

138. Despite the mixture's ________ nature, we found that by lowering its temperature in the laboratory we could dramatically reduce its tendency to vaporize.

(A) resilient

(B) volatile

(C) homogeneous

(D) insipid

(E) acerbic

139. Despite the team members' resentment of the new coach's training rules, they ________ them as long as he did not ________ them too strictly.

(A) embraced...follow

(B) condemned...formulate

(C) questioned...interpret

(D) challenged...implement

(E) tolerated...apply

140. Despite their reputations as soothing love songs sung by mothers to lull fretful infants to sleep, many lullabies are of a dark, even ________ nature.

(A) soporific

(B) manipulative

(C) threatening

(D) auspicious

(E) innocuous

141. Determined to hire employees on the basis of their merits rather than on the basis of their family connections, Johnson refused to ________ nepotism and other forms of favoritism in the engagement of new workers.

(A) obscure

(B) proscribe

(C) countenance

(D) misrepresent

(E) discern

142. Donald Trump's latest casino in Atlantic City is the most ________ gambling palace in the East, easily outglittering its competitors.

(A) professional

(B) speculative

(C) ostentatious

(D) lucrative

(E) restrained

143. Dr. Charles Drew's technique for preserving and storing blood plasma for emergency use proved so ________ that it became the ________ for the present blood bank system used by the American Red Cross.

笔记区

(A) irrelevant...inspiration
(B) urgent...pattern
(C) effective...model
(D) innocuous...excuse
(E) complex...blueprint

144. Dr. Smith cautioned that the data so far are not sufficiently ________ to warrant dogmatic assertions by either side in the debate.
(A) hypothetical
(B) tentative
(C) controversial
(D) unequivocal
(E) imponderable

145. Duke Ellington's jazz symphonies were attacked by classical critics who felt that the entire attempt to fuse jazz as a form with classical music should be ________ .
(A) promoted
(B) documented
(C) discouraged
(D) acclaimed
(E) repeated

146. During the Battle of Trafalgar, Admiral Nelson remained ________ and in full command of the situation in spite of the hysteria and panic all around him.
(A) impassable
(B) imperturbable
(C) overbearing
(D) frenetic
(E) lackadaisical

147. During the Dark Ages, hermits and other religious ________ fled the world to devote themselves to silent contemplation.
(A) renegades
(B) skeptics
(C) altruists
(D) recluses
(E) convictions

148. During the Ice Ages, muskoxen ranged as far south as Iowa, in North America, and Spain, in Europe, but in recent centuries the species has been ________ arctic tundra habitats, such as Greenland and the arctic islands of Canada.
(A) barred from
(B) confined to
(C) dissatisfied with
(D) enervated by
(E) unknown in

149. During the last four decades of Tennyson's long life, his creative powers never ________ , some

of his most remarkable work coming after the age of 70.

(A) recovered

(B) manifested

(C) flagged

(D) blossomed

(E) broadened

150. During the troubles of 1750, the ________ of Scotland was terrible; many Scots could afford nothing to eat but oatmeal porridge.

(A) anarchy

(B) reputation

(C) punishment

(D) apathy

(E) poverty

151. Egocentric, at times vindictive when he believed his authority was being questioned, White could also be kind, gracious, and even ________ when the circumstances seemed to require it.

(A) self-deprecating

(B) authoritarian

(C) provocative

(D) taciturn

(E) disdainful

152. Einstein's humility was so____ that it might have seemed a pose affected by a great man had it not been so obviously ________ .

(A) spurious...genuine

(B) convincing...assumed

(C) profound...sincere

(D) heartfelt...hypocritical

(E) modest...contrived

153. Either the Polynesian banquets at Waikiki are_____ , or the one I visited was a poor example.

(A) delicious

(B) impeccable

(C) overrated

(D) untasted

(E) unpopular

154. Either the surfing at Maui is ________ , or I went there on an off day.

(A) consistent

(B) thrilling

(C) invigorating

(D) overrated

(E) scenic

155. Elizabeth Gaskell: A Habit of Stories is a considerable ________ , superseding Winifred Gerin's learned biography of the English novelist.

(A) failure

(B) rationalization
(C) accomplishment
(D) recollection
(E) muddle

156. Even Cormac McCarthy, Don DeLillo, and William Gaddis —eminent novelists who are notoriously ________ when it comes to ________ have surrendered to the exigencies of modern publishing and agreed to be the subjects of magazine articles.
(A) prolific...writing
(B) egotistical...fame
(C) overrated...style
(D) irate...delays
(E) shy...publicity

157. Even as the local climate changed from humid to arid and back —a change that caused other animals to become extinct-our almost —human ancestors ________ by learning how to use the new flora.
(A) anticipated
(B) survived
(C) diverged
(D) deteriorated
(E) migrated

158. Even critics who do not ________ Robin Williams' interpretation of the part ________ him as an inventive comic actor who has made a serious attempt to come to terms with one of the most challenging roles of our time.
(A) dissent from...dismiss
(B) cavil at...welcome
(C) agree with...denounce
(D) recoil from...deride
(E) concur with...acknowledge

159. Even if you do not ________ what 1 have to say, I would appreciate your listening tome with an open mind.
(A) concur with
(B) reject
(C) clarify
(D) deviate from
(E) atticipate

160. Even though nonbreeding female mole rats are ________ , when the queen mole rat dies, several females suddenly ________ their sexual and reproductive powers and battle one another to replace her.
(A) prolific...accept
(B) sterile...regain
(C) barren...relinquish
(D) fecund...recover
(E) fragile...lose

笔 记 区

161. Even though the basic organization of the brain does not change after birth, details of its structure and function remain ________ for some time, particularly in the cerebral cortex.

(A) plastic
(B) immutable
(C) essential
(D) unavoidable
(E) static

162. Even when being ________ in method, people can come up with incorrect answers by basing their arguments on false premises.

(A) original
(B) logical
(C) slipshod
(D) realistic
(E) careless

163. Even while enraptured by the glorious sound produced by Miss Norman, critics ________ a certain absurdity in setting an ________ recital in the cavernous Royal Festival Hall.

(A) decried...unmelodious
(B) implied...impractical
(C) overlooked...explicit
(D) acknowledged...intimate
(E) fostered...oppressive

164. Excited and unafraid, the ________ child examined the stranger with bright-eyed curiosity.

(A) apathetic
(B) drowsy
(C) timorous
(D) inquisitive
(E) hesitant

165. Factory trawlers, large fishing vessels that drag heavy nets over the seafloor, "vacuum" the North Pacific seas, trapping fish ________ .

(A) unintentionally
(B) indiscriminately
(C) paradoxically
(D) collaboratively
(E) temporarily

166. Famed athlete Bobby Orr was given his first pair of skates by a ________ Canadian woman who somehow "knew" he would use them to attain sporting greatness.

(A) prosperous
(B) prescient
(C) notorious
(D) skeptical
(E) fallible

167. Famous in her time and then forgotten, the 17thcentury Dutch painter Judith Leyster was

笔 记 区

________ obscurity when, in 1993, the Worcester Art Museum organized the first retrospective exhibition of her work.

(A) resigned to

(B) rewarded with

(C) rescued from

(D) indifferent to

(E) worthy of

168. Far from being distracted or immobilized by his inner conflicts, Keynes was ________ by them into becoming one of the most productive, effective and buoyant personalities of the twentieth century.

(A) neutralized

(B) energized

(C) incapacitated

(D) enervated

(E) inhibited

169. Fitness experts claim that jogging is ________ ; once you begin to jog regularly, you may be unable to stop, because you are sure to love it more and more all the time.

(A) exhausting

(B) illusive

(C) addictive

(D) exotic

(E) overrated

170. Flying in the face of ________ , the writer George Sand shocked her contemporaries by taking lovers and by wearing men¡äs clothes.

(A) immodesty

(B) reconciliation

(C) emancipation

(D) convention

(E) modernism

171. For a young person, Winston seems remarkably ________; you'd expect someone his age to show a little more life.

(A) sophomoric

(B) vigorous

(C) stodgy

(D) tidy

(E) sensitive

172. For all his protestations of ________ , Judge Learned Hand had been deeply ________ at being passed over for the United States Supreme Court, where Oliver Wendell Holmes, Jr. , Benjamin Cardozo, and countless others said he belonged.

(A) innocence...embarrassed

(B) disbelief...enervated

(C) indifference...disappointed

(D) despondency...frustrated

笔 记 区

(E) affection...commiserated

173. For all of his turn-of-the-century trappings, the novel's hero is basically a ________ voice; his values and cultural ________ are of the 1990s more than the 1890s.
(A) derivative...antecedents
(B) modem...antiquity
(C) contemporary...background
(D) familiar...descendants
(E) hollow...premises

174. For all the ________ involved in the study of seals, we Arctic researchers have occasional moments of pure ________ over some new idea or discovery.
(A) tribulations...despair
(B) hardships...exhilaration
(C) confusions...bewilderment
(D) inconvenience...panic
(E) thrills...delight

175. For many years an unheralded researcher, Barbara McClintock gained international ________ when she won the Nobel Prize in Physiology and Medicine.
(A) condemnation
(B) notoriety
(C) renown
(D) affluence
(E) camaraderie

176. For someone suffering from stress, a holiday can act as a tonic, ________ rancor, transforming indecision, and renewing the spirit.
(A) enhancing
(B) exaggerating
(C) manifesting
(D) dispelling
(E) compounding

177. For those who admire realism, Louis Malle's recent film succeeds because it consciously ________ the stuff of legend and tells ________ story as it might actually unfold with fallible people in earthly time.
(A) rejects...a derivative
(B) anticipates...an antiquated
(C) shuns...an unembellished
(D) emulates...an ethereal
(E) exaggerates...a mythic

178. For years no one could make this particular therapy work in animals larger than rodents, but now two research groups have demonstrated its ________ in dogs.
(A) efficacy
(B) defects
(C) variability

笔 记 区

(D) origin
(E) virulence

179. Fortunately, she was ________ her accomplishments, properly unwilling to——them before her friends.
(A) excited by...parade
(B) immodest about...discuss
(C) deprecatory about...flaunt
(D) uncertain of...concede
(E) unaware of...conceal

180. Fossils may be set in stone, but their interpretation is not; a new find may necessitate the ________ of a traditional theory.
(A) ambiguity
(B) revision
(C) formulation
(D) validation
(E) assertion

181. From the critic's perspective, M. F. K. Fisher was a writer who ________ classification, for her food writing read like love stories, her fiction like memoirs.
(A) remembered
(B) relished
(C) skirted
(D) complied with
(E) matured with

182. From the lunch counter sit-ins and bus boycotts to the historic freedom march from Selma to Montgomery, this fine volume shows how ________ Americans from every walk of life fought ________ battle for "liberty and justice for all. "
(A) revolutionary...an unnecessary
(B) typical. . an ignoble
(C) progressive...a vainglorious
(D) ordinary...an inspiring
(E) pugnacious...a dubious

183. Gaddis is a formidably talented writer whose work has been, unhappily, more likely to intimidate or ________ his readers than to lure them into his fictional world.
(A) entice
(B) strengthen
(C) invigorate
(D) transform
(E) repel

184. Getting into street brawls is no minor matter for professional boxers, who are required by law to restrict their ________ impulses to the ring.
(A) humorous

笔 记 区

(B) aggressive
(C) obligatory
(D) amateurish
(E) legitimate

185. Given the ________ nature of wood, the oldest totem poles of the Northwest Coast Indians eventually fell to decay; only a few still stand today.
(A) resilient
(B) combustible
(C) malleable
(D) perishable
(E) solid

186. Given the ________ state of the published evidence, we do not argue here that exposure to low-level microwave energy is either hazardous or safe.
(A) inconclusive
(B) satisfactory
(C) definitive
(D) immaculate
(E) exemplary

187. Given the ability of modern technology to ________ the environment, it is clear that if we are not careful, the human race may soon be as extinct as the dinosaur.
(A) enhance
(B) destroy
(C) analyze
(D) repair
(E) nurture

188. Grateful as we are for these splendid books, they remain isolated examples of excellence in a literature of ________ .
(A) competition
(B) distinction
(C) grandeur
(D) mediocrity
(E) affirmation

189. Halls and audiences for lieder recitals tend to be smaller than for opera and thus more ________ the intimacy and sense of close involvement, which is the recital¡äs particular charm.
(A) inauspicious for
(B) destructive of
(C) conducive to
(D) compromised by
(E) indifferent to

190. Harriman, Kennan, and Acheson were part of that inner ________ of the American diplomatic establishment whose distinguished legacy ________ U. S. foreign policy to this day.
(A) circle...grieves

(B) sanctum absorbs
(C) core...dominates
(D) life...biases
(E) coterie...exacerbates

191. Having billed himself as "Mr. Clean, "Hosokawa could not ________ the ________ of a major financial scandal.
(A) survive...acclaim
(B) withstand...notoriety
(C) identify...exposure
(D) resist...charms
(E) censure...temptation

192. Having envisioned atomic weapons a decade before, Leo Szilard felt horror and guilt at the bombings of Hiroshima and Nagasaki, calling them "a flagrant ________ of our own moral standards. "
(A) violation
(B) exposition
(C) punishment
(D) vindication
(E) agitation

193. Having just published his fourth novel in an almost 40-year career, Gaddis describes himself, with some ________ , as a writer who has never been in a ________ to get into print.
(A) expectation...mood
(B) impatience...technique
(C) understatement...rush
(D) indecision...position
(E) exaggeration...school

194. Having published more than three hundred books in less than fifty years, science fiction writer Isaac Asimov may well be the most ________ author of our day.
(A) fastidious
(B) insecure
(C) outmoded
(D) prolific
(E) indigenous

195. Having recently missed out on the Matisse retrospective, which has taken Paris and New York by storm, and on the tour of great paintings from Philadelphia" Barnes collection, London is becoming ________ in the competition to show ________ international art exhibitions.
(A) a trend-setter...major
(B) an also-ran...blockbuster
(C) a world -beater...itinerant
(D) a mecca...distinguished
(E) a connoisseur...esoteric.

196. Having written 140 books to date, he may well be considered one of the most ________novelists

笔 记 区

of the century.
(A) eccentric
(B) controversial
(C) easygoing
(D) unheralded
(E) prolific

197. He continually describes what superhuman labor it has cost him tocompose his poems and ________ that, in comparison with his own work, the poetry of other poets is ________ .
(A) insists...meritorious
(B) insinuates...profound
(C) asserts...laborious
(D) intimates...superficial
(E) maintains...meticulous

198. He felt that the uninspiring routine of office work was too ________ for someone of his talent and creativity.
(A) diverse
(B) insatiable
(C) exacting
(D) enthralling
(E) prosaic

199. He found himself in the ________ position of appearing to support a point of view which he abhorred.
(A) obvious
(B) innocuous
(C) anomalous
(D) enviable
(E) auspicious

200. He has the ________ distinction of being the only one in the class to fail the examination.
(A) voluntary
(B) dubious
(C) exemplary
(D) partial
(E) logical

201. He is much too ________ in his writings: he writes a page when a sentence should suffice.
(A) devious
(B) lucid
(C) verbose
(D) efficient
(E) pleasant

202. He loved his friends, but he held people in general in ________ and maintained that human virtues were unworthy to be compared with a dog's devotion.
(A) reverence

笔 记 区

(B) abeyance
(C) contempt
(D) affection
(E) honor

203. He tried his hardest to maintain his ________ in the face of the threatening mob.
(A) synthesis
(B) analogy
(C) fraternity
(D) umbrage
(E) composure

204. He was ________ success, painting not for the sake of fame or monetary reward, but for the sheer love of art.
(A) indifferent to
(B) destined for
(C) avid for
(D) jaded by
(E) enamored of

205. He was habitually so docile and ________ that his friends could not understand his sudden ________ his employers.
(A) accommodating...outburst against
(B) incorrigible...suspicion of
(C) truculent...virulence toward
(D) erratic...envy of
(E) hasty...cordiality toward

206. He was so convinced that people were driven by ________ motives that he believed there was no such thing as a purely unselfish act.
(A) sentimental
(B) personal
(C) altruistic
(D) ulterior
(E) intrinsic

207. Helen valued people who behaved as if they respected themselves; nothing irritated her more than an excessively ________ waiter or a fawning salesclerk.
(A) austere
(B) domineering
(C) grave
(D) obsequious
(E) contentious

208. Her ________ is always a source of irritation:she never uses a single word when she can substitute a long clause or phrase in its place.
(A) frivolity
(B) verbosity

笔 记 区

(C) ambivalence
(D) cogency
(E) rhetoric

209. Her growing bitterness was ________ by her professional rivalry with her sister, whose fortunes rose while her own ________ .
(A) represented...ascended
(B) mitigated...dwindled
(C) exemplified...soared
(D) nurtured...multiplied
(E) exacerbated...declined

210. Her memoirs are quite unlike those of her predecessors, for she is bold and aggressive where they are ________ and comfortable.
(A) audacious
(B) vivid
(C) bland
(D) brazen
(E) contentious

211. Her novel published to universal acclaim, her literary gifts acknowledged by the chief figures of the Harlem Renaissance, her reputation as yet ________ by envious slights, Hurston clearly was at the ________ of her career.
(A) undamaged...ebb
(B) untarnished...zenith
(C) untainted...extremity
(D) blackened...mercy
(E) unmarred...brink

212. His critical reviews were enjoyed by many of his audience, but the subjects of his analysis dreaded his comments; he was vitriolic, devastating, irritating and never ________ .
(A) analytic
(B) personal
(C) constructive
(D) uncharitable
(E) controversial

213. His olfactory sense was so highly developed that he was often called in to judge ________ .
(A) productivity
(B) colors
(C) litigation
(D) perfume
(E) acoustics

214. His submissiveness of manner and general air of self-effacement made it ________ hewould be ________ to take command of the firm.
(A) unlikely...selected
(B) implausible...hesitant

笔 记 区

(C) clear...designated
(D) puzzling...disinclined
(E) probable...demoted

215. Hoping for a rave review of his new show, the playwright was ________ when the critics ________ is unanimously.
(A) gloomy...condoned
(B) incredulous...appraised
(C) vexed...selected
(D) miserable...panned
(E) impressed...divulged

216. Hroswitha the nun, though hidden among the cloisters and ________ time, is now considered an important literary figure of the medieval period.
(A) oppressed by
(B) fighting against
(C) celebrated throughout
(D) elapsed from
(E) obscured by

217. I am seeking an ________ solution to this dispute, one that will be fair and acceptable to both sides.
(A) equivocal
(B) infamous
(C) equitable
(D) idiosyncratic
(E) overrated

218. I can vouch for his honesty; I have always found him ________ and carefully observant of the truth.
(A) arbitrary
(B) plausible
(C) volatile
(D) veracious
(E) innocuous

219. I regret that my remarks seemed ________; I never intended to belittle you.
(A) inadequate
(B) justified
(C) unassailable
(D) disparaging
(E) shortsighted

220. If Amelia Earhart's acceptance was by no means ________, her fame was unusually widespread and her popularity long-lived.
(A) universal
(B) ambiguous
(C) expedient

(D) partial
(E) genuine

221. If you come to the conference table with such an ________ attitude, we can not expect to reach any harmonious agreement.
(A) exemplary
(B) iridescent
(C) indolent
(D) obdurate
(E) unwonted

222. If you listen carefully, you can hear this simple ________ throughout the entire score.
(A) metaphor
(B) paean
(C) banality
(D) motif
(E) trilogy

223. If you need car parts that the dealers no longer stock, try ________ for odd bits and pieces at the auto wreckers' yards.
(A) waiting
(B) bantering
(C) scavenging
(D) riveting
(E) insuring

224. If, like the mole rat, you could run backward as easily as forward but had weak eyes that could see only dim shadows of light and dark, you too might want touch-sensitive whiskers to help ________ you through the tunnels of your underground home.
(A) carry
(B) illuminate
(C) excavate
(D) distract
(E) guide

225. Illness can be ________ as how disease feels, the experience of being sick: at once a physical or natural condition and a social and cultural one.
(A) cured
(B) survived
(C) acclaimed
(D) defined
(E) deprecated

226. In Anne of Gables, the heroine turns down a prestigious scholarship so that the young hero may receive it; once more, the woman ________ her own ________ to those of the man.
(A) prefers...ambitions
(B) sacrifices...losses
(C) surrenders...talents

笔 记 区

(D) accommodates...beliefs
(E) subordinates...interests

227. In Victorian times, countless Egyptian mummies were ground up to produce dried mummy powder, hailed by quacks as a near-magical ________ able to cure a wide variety of ailments.
(A) toxin
(B) indisposition
(C) symptom
(D) panacea
(E) placebo

228. In a nation where the economic reversals of the past few years have taken a psychological as well as a financial toll on many regions, what most ________ the South may be the degree of ________ throughout the region.
(A) distinguishes...optimism
(B) grieves...prosperity
(C) typifies...disenfranchisement
(D) distresses...reflection
(E) appeases...idealism

229. In apologizing to the uncredited photographer, the editor said that he ________ that this ________ use of copyrighted photographs had taken place.
(A) deplored...legitimate
(B) conceded...inevitable
(C) regretted...unauthorized
(D) admitted...warranted
(E) acknowledged...appropriate

230. In attempting to reconcile estranged spouses, counselors try to foster a spirit of ________ rather than one of stubborn implacability.
(A) disillusionment
(B) ambivalence
(C) compromise
(D) antagonism
(E) independence

231. In discussing Rothko's art, Breslin is ________ in keeping to the facts and resisting the ________ of fanciful interpretation.
(A) scrupulous...temptation
(B) meticulous...integrity
(C) ungainly...reward
(D) uninterested...echo
(E) inept...bias

232. In giving a speech, the speaker's goal is to communicate ideas clearly and ________, so that the audience will be in no ________ about the meaning of the speech.
(A) effectively...haste
(B) indirectly...distress

笔记区

(C) vigorously...discomfort
(D) unambiguously...confusion
(E) tactfully...suspense

233. In his address, the superintendent exhorted the teachers to discover and ________ each student's ________ talents.
(A) suppress...unrecognized
(B) develop...intrinsic
(C) redirect...specious
(D) belittle...dormant
(E) justify...gratuitous

234. In judging the degree of his guilt, the question remains whether he acted out of purely ________ motives or whether he acted with thoughts of his own ________ in mind.
(A) benevolent...fame
(B) disinterested...advantage
(C) selfish...benefit
(D) mercenary...profit
(E) malicious...cleverness

235. In one instance illustrating Metternich's consuming ________, he employed several naval captains to purchase books abroad for him, eventually adding an entire Oriental library to his ________ collection.
(A) foresight...indifferent
(B) altruism...eclectic
(C) bibliomania...burgeoning
(D) avarice...inadvertent
(E) egocentricity...magnanimous

236. In prison Malcolm X set himself the task of reading straight through the dictionary; to him, reading was purposeful, not ________.
(A) deliberate
(B) retentive
(C) critical
(D) desultory
(E) exhaustive

237. In the 1920s Hollywood became a magnet for men and women on the cutting edge ________ artists genuinely excited by the possibilities of the up-and-coming film medium.
(A) irritable
(B) innovative
(C) untalented
(D) outdated
(E) inferior

238. In the absence of native predators to stop their spread, imported deer ________ to such an inordinate degree that they overgrazed the countryside and ________ the native vegetation.
(A) thrived...threatened

笔 记 区

(B) propagated...cultivated
(C) suffered...abandoned
(D) flourished...scrutinized
(E) dwindled...eliminated

239. In the constant battle for newsstand supremacy, with newsstands groaning from the weight of specialty publications, the biggest challenge facing any new magazine is ________ itself from the crowed, making its mission ________ .
(A) transforming...plausible
(B) separating...impossible
(C) distinguishing...clear
(D) acquiring...public
(E) distancing...futile

240. In the light of Dickens's description of the lively, even ________ dance parties of his time , Sharp's approach to country dancing may seem overly formal, suggesting more________ — than is necessary.
(A) sophisticated...expertise
(B) rowdy...decorum
(C) prudish...propriety
(D) lewd...ribaldry
(E) enjoyable...vitality

241. In the poem Annabel Lee, the speaker reveals that he is not ________ to the death of his beloved; on the contrary, he is ________ .
(A) indifferent...apathetic
(B) reconciled...acquiescent
(C) resigned...inconsolable
(D) accustomed...inured
(E) relevant...responsive

242. In their determination to discover ways to ________ human life, doctors fail to take into account that longer lives are not always happier ones.
(A) ease
(B) prolong
(C) eradicate
(D) recuperate
(E) dissect

243. In this survey of Revolutionary America, the author finds a remarkable homogeneity of opinion from Massachusetts to Georgia; the differences between the sections are ________ , almost always explainable by differences in climate or topography.
(A) sharp
(B) nonexistent
(C) irreconcilable
(D) superficial
(E) enormous

笔记区

244. In view of the fact that there are mitigating circumstances, we must consider this a ________ offense.
(A) heinous
(B) venal
(C) criminal
(D) propitious
(E) venial

245. In view of the interrelationships among a number of the African American leaders treated in this anthology, there is inevitably a certain amount of ________ among some of the essays presented here.
(A) overlapping
(B) inaccuracy
(C) pomposity
(D) exaggeration
(E) objectivity

246. Instead of taking exaggerated precautions against touching or tipping or jarring the bottle of wine, the waitress handled it quite ________ , being careful only to use a napkin to keep her hands from the cool bottle itself.
(A) fastidiously
(B) reverently
(C) nonchalantly
(D) tentatively
(E) ambivalently

247. Irony can, after a fashion, become a mode of escape: to laugh at the terrors of life is in some sense to ________ them.
(A) overstate
(B) revitalize
(C) corroborate
(D) evade
(E) license

248. Isozaki's love for detail is apparent everywhere in the new museum, but fortunately the details are ________ to the building¡äs larger formal composition, which is ________ by the busyness of much recent architecture.
(A) important...harmed
(B) irrelevant...fragmented
(C) subordinated...unencumbered
(D) appropriate...echoed
(E) incidental...nullified

249. It is ________ to try to destroy pests completely with chemical poisons, for as each new chemical pesticide is introduced, the insects gradually become ________ to it.
(A) useless...drawn
(B) pointless...vulnerable
(C) futile...resistant

笔 记 区

(D) wicked...indifferent

(E) worthwhile...immune

250. It is a relief to see people who can be interested in the arts without being "arty"-collectors who collect for their own ________ rather than for ________ .

(A) enjoyment...satisfaction

(B) interest...pleasure

(C) reputation...amusement

(D) delight...show

(E) education...fulfillment

25 1. It is a spotty sort of book, with many pages that, if not exactly ________ , are less than ________ .

(A) bland...tedious

(B) pretentious...conventional

(C) dull...exciting

(D) eventful...newsworthy

(E) murky...obscure

252. It is all but impossible today to ________ the ferocity with which Russian thinkers at the turn of the century ________ the materialism that had dominated their country's intellectual life since the 1850s.

(A) forget...relished

(B) believe...conceded

(C) grasp...assailed

(D) emulate...ignored

(E) challenge...extolled

253. It is possible to analyze a literary work to death, ________ what should be a living experience as if it were a laboratory specimen.

(A) questioning

(B) dissecting

(C) amending

(D) nurturing

(E) reviving

254. It is remarkable that a man so in the public eye, so highly praised and imitated, can retain his ________ .

(A) magniloquence

(B) dogmas

(C) bravado

(D) idiosyncracies

(E) humility

255. It is said that the custom of shaking hands originated when primitive men held out empty hands to indicate that they had no ________ weapons and were thus ________ disposed.

(A) lethal...clearly
(B) concealed...amicably
(C) hidden...harmfully
(D) murderous...ill
(E) secret...finally

256. It is the task of the International Wildlife Preservation Commission to prevent endangered species from becoming ________ in order that future generations may ________ the great diversity of animal life.
(A) tamed...recollect
(B) evolved...value
(C) extinct...enjoy
(D) specialized...anticipate
(E) widespread...appreciate

257. It is wise to begin to treat a progressive disease while it is still in its ________ stage.
(A) climactic
(B) clinical
(C) incipient
(D) terminal
(E) pharmaceutical

258. It was only the first day of summer vacation, but his nerves were already ________ by the constant clamor of the children.
(A) eliminated
(B) alleviated
(C) replete
(D) vacillated
(E) frayed

259. It would be beneficial if someone so radical could be brought to believe that old customs need not necessarily be ________ and that change may possibly be ________ .
(A) defensible...premature
(B) outdated...required
(C) evil...salutary
(D) invaluable...temporary
(E) worthless...inadvisable

260. Janet Malcolm depicts the biographer as a nosy, intrusive figure, ________ his subject's private papers.
(A) annotating
(B) restoring
(C) invading
(D) acknowledging
(E) compiling

261. John Gielgud crowns a distinguished career of playing Shakespearean roles by giving a performance that is ________ .

笔 记 区

(A) mediocre
(B) outmoded
(C) superficial
(D) unsurpassable
(E) insipid

262. John Keats, Dylan Thomas, Arthur Rimbaud-all these were poets who had to be poets, whom no one or nothing short of death could have ________ their courses.
(A) confirmed in
(B) derailed from
(C) lauded for
(D) interested in
(E) convinced of

263. Just as all roads once led to Rome, all blood vessels in the human body ultimately ________ the heart.
(A) detour around
(B) shut off
(C) empty into
(D) look after
(E) beat back

264. Just as an ________ dish lacks flavor, an inane remark lacks ________ .
(A) intriguing...spice
(B) insipid...sense
(C) inedible...listeners
(D) occasional...implications
(E) offensive...taste

265. Just as an orchestra cannot consist only of violins, a society cannot consist only of managers, for society is an ________ in which different parts have different ________ .
(A) anarchy...powers
(B) edifice...complaints
(C) organism...functions
(D) institution...results
(E) urbanity...ambitions

266. Just as sloth is the mark of the idler, ________is the mark of the ________ .
(A) grief...miser
(B) obsequiousness...toady
(C) wanderlust...trespasser
(D) suspicion...tyrant
(E) brevity...wit

267. Just as the earliest stone tools left by humans may seem nothing more than rock fragments to a layperson, so a lot of fossils require a trained eye to ________ them.
(A) excavate
(B) appreciate

笔 记 区

(C) disseminate
(D) antedate
(E) educate

268. Justice Harry Blackmun' s retirement, while unlikely to bring about a drastic change at the Supreme Court, will remove a distinctly ________ voice from the Court's often featureless mix.
(A) bland
(B) personal
(C) moderate
(D) neutral
(E) derivative

269. Kepler's observations of the supernova would have been more ________ and valuable had they been made with a telescope; unfortunately, Kepler's supernova lighted the night skies five full years before Galileo made the first ________ telescopic scan of the heavens.
(A) remote...skeptical
(B) solemn...unseemly
(C) infamous...extraneous
(D) detailed...documented
(E) fortuitous...recorded

270. Known for his commitment to numerous worthy causes, the philanthropist deserved ________ for his ________ .
(A) recognition...folly
(B) blame...hypocrisy
(C) reward...modesty
(D) admonishment...wastefulness
(E) credit...altruism

271. Lamenting that something horrid had recently befallen the craft of biography, biographer Arthur Schlesinger ________ the glut of gossipy new lives on the market.
(A) deplored
(B) forgot
(C) acclaimed
(D) composed
(E) abridged

272. Land is no less ________ just because it has not yet been ________ .
(A) eroded...subdivided
(B) exhausted...cultivated
(C) imaginary...discovered
(D) fallow...settled
(E) real...charted

273. Lavish in visual beauty, the film Lawrence of Arabia also boasts ________ of style: it knows how much can be shown in a shot, how much can be said in a few words.
(A) extravagance

笔 记 区

(B) economy
(C) autonomy
(D) frivolity
(E) arrogance

274. Learned though she was, her___ never degenerated into ________.
(A) erudition...pedantry
(B) knowledge...ignorance
(C) scholarship...research
(D) speculation...thought
(E) education...inquiry

275. Leavening his decisions with humorous, down-to-earth anecdotes, Judge Wapner was not at all the ________ legal scholar.
(A) considerate
(B) pedantic
(C) indecisive
(D) competent
(E) pragmatic

276. Lee, who refrained from excesses in his personal life, differed markedly from Grant, who ________ notorious drinking bouts with his cronies.
(A) deprecated
(B) minimized
(C) indulged in
(D) shunned
(E) compensated for

277. Left to endure a penniless old age, the ________ man lived to regret his ________ youth.
(A) miserly...friendless
(B) reclusive...affable
(C) eccentric...fleeting
(D) egotistical...frugal
(E) improvident...prodigal

278. Lexy's joy at finding the perfect Christmas gift for John was ________, for she still had to find presents for the cousins and Uncle Bob.
(A) transient
(B) antithetical
(C) exuberant
(D) exhaustive
(E) incontrovertible

279. Life is a ________ of the sacred and the profane, of good and evil; to ________ them is futile.
(A) rejection...embrace
(B) commingling...separate
(C) misalliance...endure
(D) defamation...reform

笔 记 区

(E) confusion...promulgate

280. Like Machiavelli before him, Henry Kissinger has a keen appreciation for the hard-headed, even ________ , use of power, to the point of admiring some traits in leaders who were otherwise ________ .

(A) cynical...benevolent
(B) gentle...insignificant
(C) ruthless. detestable
(D) resentful...charismatic
(E) forceful...exemplary

281. Like a balloon that is ________ , aneurysms (swellings in the walls of arteries) sometimes enlarge so much that they ________ .

(A) expanding...contract
(B) punctured...dilate
(C) elastic...stratify
(D) weightless...stretch
(E) overinflated...burst

282. Like a martinet, Norman ________ his subordinates to ________ rigidly to the rules.

(A) disciplined...adapt
(B) constrained...adhere
(C) coaxed...refer
(D) accustomed...object
(E) coerced...demur

283. Like doctors exploring the mysteries concealed within the human body, astronomers are finding that X rays offer an invaluable means for examining otherwise ________ structures.

(A) inconsequential
(B) hidden
(C) ambivalent
(D) diseased
(E) ephemeral

284. Like foolish people who continue to live near an active volcano, many of us are ________ about the ________ of atomic warfare and its attendant destruction.

(A) worried. . . possibility
(B) unconcerned. . . threat
(C) excited. . . power
(D) cheered. . . possession
(E) irritated. . . news

285. Like many other pioneers, Dr. Elizabeth Blackwell, founder of the New York Infirmary, the first American hospital staffed entirely by women, faced ridicule from her contemporaries but has received great honor ________ .

(A) posthumously
(B) anonymously
(C) privately

笔 记 区

(D) prematurely

(E) previously

286. Lovejoy, the hero of Jonathan Gash's mystery novels, is an antique dealer who gives the reader advice on how to tell ________ antiques from the real thing.

(A) priceless

(B) spurious

(C) classical

(D) authentic

(E) antiquated

287. MacDougall's former editors remember him as a ________ man whose ________ and exhaustive reporting was worth the trouble.

(A) domineering. . . wearisome

(B) congenial. . . pretentious

(C) popular. . . supercilious

(D) fastidious. . . garbled

(E) cantankerous. . . meticulous

288. Many educators argue that a ________ grouping of students would improve instruction because it would limit the range of student abilities in the classroom.

(A) heterogeneous

(B) systematic

(C) homogeneous

(D) sporadic

(E) fragmentary

289. Many elderly people are capable of working, but they are kept from gainful employment by the ________ of those employers who mistakenly believe that young people alone can give them adequate service.

(A) philosophy

(B) parsimony

(C) conservatism

(D) rationalizations

(E) short-sightedness

290. Many of the early Hollywood moguls sought to ________ themselves and enhance their celluloid empires by snaring ________ writers and intellectuals as screenwriters.

(A) advance...presumptuous

(B) aggrandize...prestigious

(C) intimidate...unsuspecting

(D) glorify...superannuated

(E) sabotage...distinguished

291. Many scientific discoveries are a matter of ________ : Newton was not sitting there thinking about gravity when the apple dropped on his head.

(A) serendipity

(B) experimentation

笔 记 区

(C) casuistry

(D) technology

(E) principle

292. Marketing specialists have begun ________ what had once been a ________ audience into innumerable segments based on age, sex, income, and a host of pop sociological categories.

(A) carving up...mass

(B) bringing together...fragmented

(C) tearing apart...sophisticated

(D) unifying...distinct

(E) transforming...responsive

293. Micawber's habit of spending more than he earned left him in a state of perpetual ________ , but he ________ hoping to see a more affluent day.

(A) indigence...persevered in

(B) confusion...compromised by

(C) enervation...retaliated by

(D) motion...responded by

(E) opulence...insisted on

294. Mindful that his hardworking parents ________ to give him an education, Lopez, now wealthy, contributes to scholarship funds for the needy.

(A) planned...needlessly

(B) skimped...profitable

(C) squandered...sparingly

(D) struggled...generously

(E) regaled...regretfully

295. Morphing is a term________ for the metamorphosis of one shape into another, such as the smooth formation of a live actor from a silvery puddle as seen in Terminator 2.

(A) coined

(B) denigrated

(C) simulated

(D) mistaken

(E) repudiated

296. Most Antarctic animals ________ depend on the tiny shrimplike krill, either feeding on them directly, like the humpback whale, or consuming species that feed on them.

(A) seldom

(B) ultimately

(C) preferably

(D) immediately

(E) marginally

297. Most of the settlements that grew up near the logging camps were ________ affairs, thrown together in a hurry because people needed to live on the job.

(A) protracted

(B) unobtrusive

(C) nomadic
(D) ramshackle
(E) banal

298. Most people who are color-blind actually can distinguish several colors; some, however, have a truly ________ view of a world all in shades of gray.
(A) monochromatic
(B) opalescent
(C) translucent
(D) astigmatic
(E) roseate

299. Mr. Levi is ________ learned; he has read everything bearing on his subject and on poetry in general (in several languages) , and he has forgotten little if anything.
(A) moderately
(B) spottily
(C) inadvertently
(D) formidably
(E) inadequately

300. Mrs. Thatcher had a better eye for the weaknesses and ________ of her contemporaries than for their virtues.
(A) responsibilities
(B) foibles
(C) merits
(D) talents
(E) attractions

301. Ms. Ono ________ gives interviews because she believes the news media have ________ her and treated her badly.
(A) frequently...publicized
(B) rarely...misrepresented
(C) seldom...eulogized
(D) reluctantly...acclaimed
(E) gradually...evaded

302. Much of the clown's success may be attributed to the contrast between the ________ manner he adopts and the general ________ that characterizes the circus.
(A) giddy...sobriety
(B) lugubrious...hilarity
(C) gaudy...clamor
(D) joyful...hysteria
(E) frenetic...excitement

303. Muskoxen survived in isolated arctic habitats, but in the nineteenth century, they declined rapidly even there, their numbers ________ by the armed enthusiasm of explorers, whalers, fur traders, and Eskimo.
(A) swelled

(B) augmented
(C) devastated
(D) underestimated
(E) calculated

304. New Yorker short stories often include _____ allusions to______ people and events:the implication is, if you are in the incrowd, you'll get the reference; if youcome from Cleveland, you won't.
(A) esoteric...obscure
(B) redundant...celebrated
(C) tedious. . notorious
(D) provincial...major
(E) passing...common

305. New judges often fear that the influence of their own backgrounds will ________ their verdicts, no matter how sincere they are in wanting to be ________ .
(A) contradict...revered
(B) corroborate...silent
(C) condition...impartial
(D) disclose...secretive
(E) falsify...humane

306. No matter how ________ the revelations of the coming years may be, they will be hard put to match those of the past decade, which have ________ transformed our view of the emergence of Mayan civilization.
(A) minor...dramatically
(B) profound...negligibly
(C) striking...radically
(D) bizarre...nominally
(E) questionable...possibly

307. No real life hero of ancient or modern days can surpass James Bond with his nonchalant ________ of death and the ________ with which he bears torture.
(A) contempt...distress
(B) disregard...fortitude
(C) veneration. . . guile
(D) concept...terror
(E) ignorance...fickleness

308. No summary of the behavior of animals toward reflected images is given, but not much else that is ________ seems missing from this comprehensive yet compact study of mirrors and mankind.
(A) redundant
(B) contemplative
(C) relevant
(D) peripheral
(E) disputable

309. Now better known for its racetrack, Saratoga Springs first gained attention for the ________

笔 记 区

qualities of its famous "healing waters. "

(A) diagnostic

(B) commercial

(C) therapeutic

(D) overlooked

(E) experimental

310. Nowadays life models—men and women who pose in the nude for artists—seem curiously ________ , relics of a bygone age when art students labored amid skeletons and anatomical charts, learning to draw the human body as painstakingly as medical students learn to ________ it.

(A) anachronistic. . . sketch

(B) archaic. . . dissect

(C) contemporary. . . diagnose

(D) stereotyped. . . examine

(E) daring. . . cure

311. Numerous studies have found that people who choose to represent themselves in court on the whole exercise pretty good judgment-they seem to have a ________ sense of when they need a lawyer and when they don't.

(A) faulty

(B) capricious

(C) reliable

(D) transient

(E) drastic

312. On some occasions Monteverdi specifies the instruments he wishes to make up his orchestra, but more often he is ________ or silent on the issue.

(A) enigmatic

(B) precise

(C) eloquent

(D) resolute

(E) vehement

313. One by one, she ________ almost all of her supporters until, at the end, only a handful of her closest allies really wanted her to stay in office.

(A) promoted

(B) alienated

(C) represented

(D) exaggerated

(E) liberated

314. One might dispute the author's handling of particular points of Kandinsky's interaction with his artistic environment, but her main theses are ________ .

(A) unaesthetic

(B) incongruous

(C) untenable

(D) undecipherable

笔 记 区

(E) irreproachable

315. One of Detroit's great success stories tells of Lee lacocca's revitalization of the moribund Chrysler Corporation, turning it into a ________ competitor.

(A) vigorous
(B) tentative
(C) marginal
(D) negligent
(E) superficial

316. One of photography's most basic and powerful traits is its ability to give substance to ________, to present precise visual details of a time gone by.

(A) romance
(B) premonition
(C) mysticism
(D) invisibility
(E) history

317. One of the great killers until barely 50 years ago, tuberculosis ("consumption" ________ as it was then named) seemed a scourge or ________ rather than the long-term ________ illness it was.

(A) plague...chronic
(B) detriment...ominous
(C) antiseptic...prevalent
(D) vestige...contemporary
(E) epidemic...salutary

318. Only the fear of immediate ________ prevents that country from launching an attack.

(A) reprisal
(B) surrender
(C) truce
(D) surveillance
(E) rebuke

319. Our mood swings about the economy grow more extreme: when things go well, we become ________ ; when things go poorly, ________ descends.

(A) restive...anxiety
(B) euphoric...gloom
(C) prudent...benevolence
(D) ascetic...misery
(E) ambivalence...optimism

320. Pain is the body's early warning system:loss of ________ in the extremities leaves a person injuring himself unwittingly.

(A) agony...in capable of
(B) sensation...vulnerable to
(C) consciousness...desirous of
(D) feeling...habituated to

(E) movement...prone to

321. Paradoxically, Helen, who had been a strict mother to her children, proved ________ mistress to her cats.
(A) a harsh
(B) an indolent
(C) an ambivalent
(D) a cautious
(E) a lenient

322. Paradoxically, while it is relatively easy to prove a fraudulent work of art is a fraud, it is often virtually impossible to prove that an authentic one is ________ .
(A) unpretentious
(B) objective
(C) impartial
(D) dubious
(E) genuine

323. People expected Winston Churchill to take his painting lightly, but Churchill, no ________ , regarded his artistic efforts most seriously indeed.
(A) virtuoso
(B) zealot
(C) dilettante
(D) altruist
(E) renegade

324. People who don't outgrow their colleges often don't grow in other ways; there remained in Forster's life and imagination a ________ of the undergraduate, clever but ________
(A) dislike...talented
(B) touch...judicious
(C) streak...immature
(D) fear...dormant
(E) trace...sincere

325. People who take megadoses of vitamins and minerals should take care: though beneficial in small quantities, in large amounts these substances may have ________ effects.
(A) admirable
(B) redundant
(C) intangible
(D) toxic
(E) minor

326. Perhaps because he feels ________ by an excess of parental restrictions and rules, at adolescence the repress child may break out dramatically.
(A) nurtured
(B) appeased
(C) confined
(D) fascinated

笔 记 区

(E) liberated

327. Peter has a bad habit of making ________ remarks that cause us to forget the gist of what he is saying.
(A) awkward
(B) pertinent
(C) digressive
(D) telling
(E) tentative

328. Physicists dream of a unified theory of matter that could replace the present ________ of mutually in consistent theories that litter the field.
(A) bonanza
(B) concord
(C) dearth
(D) integration
(E) clutter

329. Polls indicate that many prospective voters in the next presidential election are ________ about the outcome; they do not seemto care who wins.
(A) enthusiastic
(B) inadequate
(C) antagonistic
(D) apathetic
(E) suspicious

330. Pre-Spanish art in Mexico is not a ________ art; they are mistaken who see in its bold simplifications or wayward conceptions an inability to ________ technical difficulties.
(A) formal...ignore
(B) graphic...understand
(C) primitive...nurture
(D) crude...overcome
(E) revolutionary...instigate

331. Precision of wording is necessary in good writing; by choosing words that exactly convey the desired meaning, one can avoid ________ .
(A) redundancy
(B) complexity
(C) duplicity
(D) ambiguity
(E) lucidity

332. Publishers have discovered that black America is not a ________ of attitudes and opinions but a rich mixture lending itself to numerous expressions in print.
(A) concoction
(B) medley
(C) monolith
(D) paradox

笔 记 区

(E) controversy

333. Quick-breeding and immune to most pesticides, cockroaches are so ________ that even a professional exterminator may fail to ________ them.

(A) vulnerable. . . eradicate

(B) widespread. . . discern

(C) fragile. . . destroy

(D) hardy. . . eliminate

(E) numerous. . . detect

334. Rather than allowing these dramatic exchanges between her characters to develop fully, Ms. Norman unfortunately tends to ________ the discussions involving the two women.

(A) exacerbate

(B) protract

(C) truncate

(D) augment

(E) elaborate

335. Rebuffed by his colleagues, the initially ________ young researcher became increasingly ________.

(A) outgoing...withdrawn

(B) boisterous...excitable

(C) diligent...tolerant

(D) theoretical...pragmatic

(E) tedious...polished

336. Rent control restrictions on small apartment owners may unfortunately ________ rather than alleviate housing problems.

(A) resolve

(B) diminish

(C) castigate

(D) minimize

(E) exacerbate

337. Repeat offenders who continue to drive under the influence of alcohol face having their drivers' licenses permanently ________.

(A) issued

(B) recorded

(C) authorized

(D) revoked

(E) disregarded

338. Rosa was such a last-minute worker that she could never start writing a paper till the deadline was ________.

(A) known

(B) problematic

(C) imminent

(D) superseded

笔 记 区

(E) recent

339. Safire as a political commentator is patently never ________ ; he writes ________ editorials about every action the government takes.
(A) content. . . deferential
(B) querulous. . . biased
(C) amazed. . . bemused
(D) overawed. . . flattering
(E) satisfied. . . peevish

340. Salvador Dali's tendency to fabricate events makes it difficult for the biographer to tell the story of his life with any degree of ________ .
(A) vividness
(B) accuracy
(C) solemnity
(D) spontaneity
(E) artistry

341. Samuel Johnson gave more than ________ cooperation to his biographer, James Boswell; he made himself available to Boswell night after night, furnished Boswell with correspondence, even read his biographer's notes.
(A) innocuous
(B) collusive
(C) tacit
(D) edifying
(E) diplomatic

342. Satisfied that her name had been ________ , she dropped her libel suit after the newspaper finally published a ________ of its originaldefamatory statement.
(A) praised...summary
(B) maligned...glossary
(C) vindicated...repetition
(D) enhanced...reaffirmation
(E) cleared...retraction

343. Science is always ________ , expecting that modifications of its present theories will sooner or later be found necessary.
(A) conclusive
(B) irrefutable
(C) original
(D) tentative
(E) inflexible

344. Science progresses by building on what has come before; important findings thus form the basis of ________ experiments.
(A) gradual
(B) subsequent
(C) ingenious

(D) repetitive
(E) perfunctory

345. Shakespeare's reference to clocks in "Julius Caesar" is an example of ________ ' that is, it is chronologically out of place.
(A) timeliness
(B) antiquarianism
(C) anachronism
(D) synchronization
(E) ignorance

346. She ________ recognition and fame, yet she felt a deep suspicion and ________ for the world in which recognition and fame are granted, the world of money and opinion and power.
(A) mistrusted...antagonism
(B) worked for...respect
(C) endured...veneration
(D) shunned...enmity
(E) yearned for...contempt

347. She has sufficient tact to ________ the ordinary crises of diplomatic life; however, even her diplomacy is insufficient to enable her to ________ the current emergency.
(A) negotiate. . . comprehend
(B) survive. . . exaggerate
(C) handle. . . weather
(D) ignore. . . transform
(E) aggravate. . . resolve

348. She is an interesting ________ , an infinitely shy person who, in apparent contradiction, possesses an enormously intuitive ________ for understanding people.
(A) aberration disdain
(B) caricature...talent
(C) specimen...loathing
(D) phenomenon...disinclination
(E) paradox...gift

349. She kept her late parents' furniture, not for any ________ value it had, but for purely ________ reasons.
(A) potential. . . monetary
(B) ornamental. . . aesthetic
(C) financial. . . pecuniary
(D) intrinsic. . . sentimental
(E) personal. . . accidental

350. She maintained that the proposed legislation was ________ because it simply established an affirmative action task force without making any appropriate provision to fund such a force.
(A) inevitable
(B) inadequate

笔 记 区

(C) prudent
(D) necessary
(E) beneficial

351. She pointed out that his resume was ________ because it merely recorded his previous positions and failed to highlight the specific skills he had mastered in each job.
(A) disinterested
(B) inadequate
(C) conclusive
(D) obligatory
(E) detailed

352. She was accused of plagiarism in a dispute over a short story, and, though ________, she never recovered from the accusation and the scandal.
(A) indicted
(B) verified
(C) exonerated
(D) retaliated
(E) convinced

353. She was pleased by the accolades she received; like everyone else, she enjoyed being ________.
(A) entertained
(B) praised
(C) playful
(D) vindicated
(E) charitable

354. She wondered whether triangles, which had only three sides, ________ as polygons, which she thought of as many-sided.
(A) theorized
(B) estimated
(C) qualified
(D) subsisted
(E) multiplied

355. Since novelty of presentation is apt to add to a performer's popularity, the most successful troubadours were those who were also the most ________ in their delivery.
(A) spontaneous
(B) lyrical
(C) academic
(D) practiced
(E) repetitious

356. Skulls are the Rosetta stones of anthropology, because they bear unique features that let scientists ________ whether two fossil samples come from the same type of creature.
(A) determine
(B) prophesy

(C) disregard
(D) initiate
(E) recollect

357. So important was the textile trade between England and America ________ quantities of indigo and raw-ginned cotton a year going in one direction, millions of yards of printed cotton fabrics in the other ________ that it ________ right through the American War of Independence.
(A) immense...innovated
(B) vast...continued
(C) illicit...collaborated
(D) insignificant...diversified
(E) enormous...ceased

358. Some spiderwebs are sheets or tangles of threads that delay the ________ of prey, allowing the spider, ________ by vibrations that travel through the threads, time to make its way over to the entangled victim.
(A) escape...alerted
(B) consumption...frightened
(C) capture...thwarted
(D) pursuit...soothed
(E) sighting...irritated

359. Some thought Dali was a brilliant painter; others ________ him as a conceited poseur.
(A) respected
(B) venerated
(C) dismissed
(D) vindicated
(E) exasperated

360. Something in Christopher responded to the older man's air of authority; he looked ________ , used to ________ .
(A) magisterial...command
(B) monumental...intimidate
(C) diffident...domineer
(D) masterful...obey
(E) decisive...fret

361. Strindberg's plays are marked by his extreme ________ ; he felt modem woman needed to ________ man and by subordinating him invalidate his masculinity.
(A) acrimony...comfort
(B) misogyny...dominate
(C) hypocrisy...reinvigorate
(D) philosophy...abstract
(E) altruism...civilize

362. Stunned by Professor Marian Diamond's work showing how the rat brain structure can increase by 5 to 7 percent, one ________ neuroanatomist stated flatly, "Young lady, that brain cannot ________ !"

笔 记 区

(A) astounded...function
(B) aghast...deteriorate
(C) dumbfounded...think
(D) skeptical...grow
(E) finicky...die

363. Such an ________ act of hostility can only lead to war.
(A) erratic
(B) occasional
(C) overt
(D) isolated
(E) anticlimactic

364. Such was Brandon's ________ that he was at times described as being honest as the day was long.
(A) vigilance
(B) munificence
(C) probity
(D) gravity
(E) eminence

365. Sue felt that Jack's ________ in the face of the compelling evidence which she had presented was an example of his ________ mind.
(A) truculence...unbiased
(B) skepticism...open
(C) incredulity...closed
(D) acquiescence...keen
(E) reluctance...impartial

366. Supporters of the proposed waterway argue that it will ________ rather than ________ railroad facilities, since the waterway will be icebound during the only months when the railroads can absorb much traffic.
(A) limit...extend
(B) build...destroy
(C) weaken...help
(D) surpass...equal
(E) supplement...threaten

367. Surprisingly enough, it is more difficult to write about the ________ than about the ________ and strange.
(A) specific. . . foreign
(B) abstract. . . prosaic
(C) commonplace. . . exotic
(D) simple. . . routine
(E) ludicrous. . . dejected

368. Surrounded by a host of besiegers and unable to ________ their supplies, the defenders of the castle feared their food would soon be ________.
(A) replenish. . . exhausted

笔 记 区

(B) consume. . . hoarded
(C) replace. . . obtainable
(D) estimate. . . superfluous
(E) deplete. . . rationed

369. Surrounded by a retinue of sycophants who invariably ________ her singing, Callas wearied of the constant adulation and longed for honest criticism.
(A) orchestrated
(B) thwarted
(C) assailed
(D) extolled
(E) reciprocated

370. T. S. Eliot, famous for his ________ , nevertheless accepted posterity's interest in his life, ________ that his correspondence with his lady friends eventually would be read.
(A) reticence...assuming
(B) modesty...prohibiting
(C) boastfulness...remembering
(D) vanity...intimating
(E) curiosity...regretting

371. Tacitus' descriptions of Germanic tribal customs were ________ by the ________ state of communications in his day, but they match the accounts of other contemporary writers.
(A) defined. . . inconsequential
(B) limited. . . primitive
(C) enriched. . . antiquated
(D) contradicted. . . thriving
(E) muddled. . . suspended

372. Telling gripping tales about a central character engaged in a mighty struggle with events, modern biographies satisfy the American appetite for ________ narratives.
(A) lyrical
(B) colloquial
(C) digressive
(D) undemanding
(E) epic

373. Thanks to the emerging technology of active noise control, automakers may soon be able to ________ noise inside a car and create the long-promised "quiet ride. "
(A) dampen
(B) energize
(C) undertake
(D) concentrate
(E) augment

374. That Mr. Willis's newest film is No. 1 at the box office this week is a testament to the star's ________ power and not to the reviews, which were ________ at best.
(A) waning. . . indifferent

笔记区

(B) ongoing. . . glowing
(C) drawing. . . modest
(D) increasing. . . matchless
(E) unique. . . superb

375. That the brain physically changes when stimulated, instead of remaining ________ from infancy to death, as previously thought, was Doctor Marian Diamond's first, and perhaps most far reaching discovery.
(A) mutable
(B) static
(C) sensory
(D) vigorous
(E) fluid

376. The ________ ambassador was but ________ linguist; yet he insisted on speaking to foreign dignitaries in their own tongues without resorting to a translator's aid.
(A) eminent. . . an indifferent
(B) visiting. . . a notable
(C) revered. . . a talented
(D) distinguished. . . a celebrated
(E) ranking. . . a sensitive

377. The ________ in the Bible are both entertaining and instructive.
(A) syllables
(B) abatements
(C) milestones
(D) parables
(E) utilities

378. The ________ of such utopian notions is reflected by the quick disintegration of theidealistic community at Brooke Farm.
(A) timeliness
(B) creativity
(C) impracticability
(D) effervescence
(E) vindication

379. The ________, by definition, possesses wisdom; the virtuoso, by definition, possesses ________.
(A) scholar...morality
(B) sage...expertise
(C) zealot...sincerity
(D) visionary...idealism
(E) pedant...proficiency

380. The Americans and the British seem to have a dog-in-the-manger attitude toward the island of Malta, no longer needing it themselves but nevertheless wishing to ________ it to others.
(A) interpret
(B) offer

笔 记 区

(C) deny
(D) praise
(E) reveal

381. The Apache are a ________ society, where husbands typically move into wives' dwellings and women take the leadership role in family affairs.
(A) sedentary
(B) defunct
(C) fragmented
(D) matrilineal
(E) xenophobic

382. The Battle of Lexington was not, as most of us have been taught, a ________ rising of individual farmers, but was instead a tightly organized, well-planned event.
(A) premeditated
(B) cautionary
(C) spontaneous
(D) coordinated
(E) theoretical

383. The Cabinet member's resignation was not a total ________ : rumors of his imminent departure had been making the rounds in Washington for a week.
(A) withdrawal
(B) success
(C) shock
(D) eclipse
(E) pretense

384. The TV news magazine sits precisely at the ________ of information and entertainment, for while it is not a silly sitcom, it is not a documentary either.
(A) foundation
(B) juncture
(C) cessation
(D) institution
(E) eclipse

385. The Turner Network's new production is an absorbing Heart of Darkness, watchful, surreptitious, almost ________ as it waits to ________ our emotions.
(A) lighthearted...cater to
(B) melancholy...cheer up
(C) mercenary...pay for
(D) predatory...pounce on
(E) furtive...figure out

386. The abundance and diversity of insects is the cumulative effect of an extraordinarily low ________ rate: bugs endure.
(A) metabolic
(B) density

(C) extinction
(D) percentage
(E) standard

387. The actor's stories of backstage feuds and rivalry might be thought ________ were there not so many corroborating anecdotes from other theatrical personalities.
(A) pantomime
(B) ambiguity
(C) approbation
(D) hyperbole
(E) vainglory

388. The advocates of anarchy are ignoring the ________ such a form of government will bring with it.
(A) chaos
(B) restrictions
(C) advantages
(D) renewal
(E) compromises

389. The amusements of modern urban people tend more and more to be ________ and to consist of the ________ of the skilled activities of others.
(A) strenuous...contemplation
(B) healthful...enjoyment
(C) solitary...sharing
(D) passive...observation
(E) intellectual...repetition

390. The aorta is like a tree trunk from which other major arteries ________ .
(A) escape
(B) subtract
(C) clamber down
(D) branch off
(E) strip away

391. The articles that he wrote ran the gamut from the serious to the lighthearted, from objective to the ________ , from the innocuous to the ________ .
(A) constant...evil
(B) casual...realistic
(C) ridiculous...remote
(D) argumentative...hostile
(E) incapacitated...conditioned

392. The artists of the Chinese avant-garde have used Western styles ________ and meaningfully to accomplish artistic ends of their own.
(A) obsequiously
(B) shamefully
(C) cannily

笔 记 区

(D) fortuitously
(E) problematically

393. The attorney's vibrant voice and ________ sense of timing were as useful to him as his prodigious preparation, attention to detail, and ________ of the law.
(A) deficient...conception
(B) excellent...ignorance
(C) shaky...command
(D) outstanding...mastery
(E) impeccable...deprecation

394. The audience failed to warm to the candidate, whose speech contained nothing but empty promises, ________ , and cliches.
(A) candor
(B) platitudes
(C) nuances
(D) ingenuity
(E) threats

395. The bank teller's ________ of the funds was not discovered until the auditors examined the accounts.
(A) extradition
(B) embezzlement
(C) patronage
(D) subordination
(E) verification

396. The benefits of telecommuting-working at home by means of various electronic communication devices rather than ________ commuting to an office-have been so clearly and consistently ________ that telework is on the rise in virtually every country with a functioning telephone system.
(A) personally...forgotten
(B) instantly...underrated
(C) physically...demonstrated
(D) painfully...denounced
(E) intermittently...discredited

397. The best Eskimo carvings of all ages seem to possess a powerful ability to ________ the great barriers of language and time and communicate ________ with us.
(A) leap over...temporarily
(B) reach across...directly
(C) rise above...verbally
(D) pass through...infrequently
(E) leave behind...anonymously

398. The biochemistry instructor urged that we take particular care of the ________ chemicals to prevent their evaporation.
(A) insoluble

笔 记 区

(B) superficial
(C) extraneous
(D) volatile
(E) insipid

399. The biographer may not have ________ the depths of her subject's self-contradictory character, but she has traced its intriguingly complex ________ .
(A) plumbed...tedium
(B) sounded...surface
(C) thwarted...background
(D) reached...insipidity
(E) disregarded...psyche

400. The biographer of Tennyson is confronted with the problem, rarely solved, of how to make a basically ________ life interesting.
(A) dramatic
(B) bewildering
(C) intriguing
(D) controversial
(E) uneventful

401. The book will arouse antagonism, disagreement, and animosity among theologians because it will ________ many ________ rituals and beliefs.
(A) undermine...iconoclastic
(B) tolerate...accepted
(C) disturb...established
(D) disregard...forgotten
(E) observe...pious

402. The campus police who monitored the demonstrations had little respect for the student protesters, generally speaking of them in ________ terms.
(A) hyperbolic
(B) euphemistic
(C) pejorative
(D) derivative
(E) uncertain

403. The child needed physical therapy to ________ the rigidity that had tragically immobilized his legs.
(A) prescribe
(B) protract
(C) counteract
(D) accentuate
(E) restore

404. The civil rights movement did not emerge from obscurity into national prominence overnight; on the contrary, it captured the public's imagination only ________ .
(A) fruitlessly

笔 记 区

(B) unimpeachably
(C) momentarily
(D) expeditiously
(E) gradually

405. The college librarian initiated a new schedule of fines for overdue books with the ________, if not the outright encouragement, of the faculty library committee.
(A) skepticism
(B) acquiescence
(C) scorn
(D) applause
(E) disapprobation

406. The college president made the ________ statement that no student athlete on academic probation, not even the topscorer of the varsity team, would be allowed to participate in intercollegiate sports.
(A) impertinent
(B) uncontroversial
(C) opinionated
(D) categorical
(E) equivocal

407. The columnist was almost ________ when he mentioned his friends, but he was unpleasant and even ________ when he discussed people who irritated him.
(A) recalcitrant. . . laconic
(B) reverential. . . acrimonious
(C) sensitive. . . remorseful
(D) insipid. . . militant
(E) benevolent. . . stoical

408. The commission of inquiry censured the senator for his ________ expenditure of public funds, which they found to be ________.
(A) flagrant...cursory
(B) improper...vindicated
(C) lavish...unjustifiable
(D) judicious...blameworthy
(E) arbitrary...critical

409. The contract negotiations were often surprisingly ________, deteriorating at times into a welter of accusations and counter-accusations.
(A) perspicacious
(B) phlegmatic
(C) sedate
(D) acrimonious
(E) propitious

410. The critics were distressed that an essayist of such glowing ________ could descend to writing such dull, uninteresting prose.

(A) obscurity
(B) ill-repute
(C) shallowness
(D) promise
(E) amiability

411. The developing brain can be likened to a highway system that ________ use: less traveled roads may be abandoned, popular roads broadened, and new ones added where they are needed.
(A) suffers from
(B) evolves with
(C) detours around
(D) atrophies with
(E) buckles under

412. The discovery by George Poinar and Roberta Hess that amber could preserve intact tissue from million-year-old insects________ the possibility, since proved correct, that it also could preserve intact DNA.
(A) eliminated
(B) distorted
(C) raised
(D) precluded
(E) predestined

413. The dispute became so ________ that we were afraid the adversaries would come to blows.
(A) ironic
(B) generalized
(C) didactic
(D) articulate
(E) acrimonious

414. The eighteenth century was a kind of golden age in deaf history because with the establishment of deaf schools, deaf people emerged from ________ and began to appear in positions of eminence and ________ as writers, engineers, philosophers, and intellectuals.
(A) retirement...ambiguity
(B) seclusion...compromise
(C) obscurity...responsibility
(D) hiding...ignominy
(E) solicitude...disrepute

415. The enemy soldiers were hot in pursuit; desperate, the fugitive sought ________ in the village church.
(A) salvation
(B) sanctuary
(C) confirmation
(D) therapy
(E) repudiation

416. The faculty senate warned that, if its recommendations were to go unheeded, the differences

between the administration and the teaching staff would be ________ and eventually rendered irreconcilable.

(A) rectified

(B) exacerbated

(C) imponderable

(D) eradicated

(E) alienated

417. The fire marshalls spend many hours seeking the cause of the ________ in which so many people were killed and so many others hospitalized with major bums.

(A) maelstrom

(B) labyrinth

(C) conflagration

(D) torpor

(E) carnage

418. The governor's imposition of martial law on the once-peaceful community was the last straw, so far as the lawmakers were concerned: the legislature refused to function until martial law was ________ .

(A) reaffirmed

(B) reiterated

(C) inaugurated

(D) rescinded

(E) prolonged

419. The guerrillas were so ________ that the general had to develop various strategies to trap them.

(A) distant

(B) wild

(C) unreasonable

(D) elusive

(E) cruel

420. The herb Chinese parsley is an example of what we mean by an acquired taste:Westerners who originally ________ it eventually come to ________ its flavor in Oriental foods.

(A) relish. . . enjoy

(B) dislike. . . welcome

(C) savor. . . abhor

(D) ignore. . . detest

(E) discern. . . recognize

421. The heretofore peaceful natives, seeking ________ the treachery of their supposed allies, became, ________ enough according to their perspective, embittered and vindictive.

(A) acquiescence in. . . understandably

(B) magnanimity towards. . . logically

(C) evidence of. . . impartially

(D) retribution for. . . justifiably

(E) exoneration of. . . ironically

笔 记 区

422. The humorist Mark Twain had a great ________ for history and historians, observing that each year the antiquarians shed new darkness on the past.
(A) reverence
(B) affinity
(C) tolerance
(D) contempt
(E) empathy

423. The hypocrite______ feelings which he does not possess but which he feels he should display.
(A) conceals
(B) decries
(C) betrays
(D) simulates
(E) condones

424. The idea that people are basically economic creatures, intent only upon their own material advantage, induces disbelief in the ________ of any ________ motive.
(A) purpose...natural
(B) desirability...ulterior
(C) stupidity...altruistic
(D) seemliness...egoistic
(E) integrity...unselfish

425. The incidence of smoking among women, formerly ________ , has grown to such a degree that lung cancer, once a minor problem, has become the chief ________ of cancer-related deaths among women,
(A) negligible. . . cause
(B) minor. . antidote
(C) preeminent. . . cure
(D) relevant. . . modifier
(E) pervasive. . . opponent

426. The increasingly popular leader of America's second largest tribe, Cherokee Chief Wilma Mankiller, has ________ the myth that only males could be leaders in American Indian government.
(A) shattered
(B) perpetuated
(C) exaggerated
(D) confirmed
(E) venerated

427. The jazz musician cannot play well if he is completely ________ , as if lying half asleep in a Jacuzzi.
(A) untruthful
(B) autonomous
(C) sincere
(D) relaxed
(E) talented

笔 记 区

428. The late James Beard was ________ with his time and knowledge-a ________ trait in the narrow world of food writing, a milieu notorious for its pettiness and infighting.
(A) unselfish...common
(B) unconcerned...standard
(C) stingy...remarkable
(D) occupied...negative
(E) generous...rare

429. The likenesses of language around the Mediterranean were sufficiently marked to ________ ease of movement both of men and ideas: it took relatively few alterations to make a Spanish song intelligible in Italy, and an Italian trader could, without much difficulty, make himself at home in France.
(A) eliminate
(B) facilitate
(C) hinder
(D) clarify
(E) aggravate

430. The linguistic ________ of refugee children is ________ their readiness to adopt the language of their new homeland.
(A) conservatism. . . indicated by
(B) inadequacy. . . demonstrated by
(C) adaptability. . . reflected in
(D) philosophy. . . contradicted by
(E) structure. . . equivalent to

431. The low-cost apartment buildings, new and well managed, are ________ to those accustomed to living in tenements_____ by shady characters.
(A) a boon...haunted
(B) a specter...inhabited
(C) an exodus...frequented
(D) an example...viewed
(E) a surprise...approached

432. The marketers' ________ in donating the new basketball backboards to the school system are not solely ________ ; they plan to sell advertising space on the backboards. turning them into miniature billboards.
(A) losses...obvious
(B) expectations...peculiar
(C) aims...mercenary
(D) reasons...sensitive
(E) motivations...philanthropic

433. The mayor and school superintendent let their dispute over budget cuts_____ to ugly and destructive proportions.
(A) escalate
(B) automate
(C) stagnate

笔 记 区

(D) condense
(E) dwindle

434. The members of the Better Government League vowed to ________ all traces of ________ between criminals and politicians.
(A) exterminate. . . controversy
(B) instigate. . . contact
(C) abhor. . . animosity
(D) eradicate. . . collusion
(E) impound. . . ties

435. The moon was hidden and the night had grown very dark; she had to ________ to see.
(A) blink
(B) strain
(C) mask
(D) remember
(E) reflect

436. The most consistent qualities of Forster's novels are the human isolation and passivity in them; his principal characters stand slightly apart and ________ , but rarely ________
(A) sneer...collapse
(B) interact...adapt
(C) mourn...recollect
(D) observe...act
(E) domineer...participate

437. The most crucial issue for wildlife in this arid land is unimpeded____ water.
(A) passage through
(B) freedom from
(C) access to
(D) saturation in
(E) overflow of

438. The museum administration appears to be singularly ________ the comforts of its employees, providing an employee health club, a lending library, and a part-time social worker to help staff members with financial or domestic problems.
(A) ignorant of
(B) indifferent to
(C) attentive to
(D) exploited by
(E) uninvolved in

439. The museum arranged the fossils in ________ order, placing the older fossils dating from the Late Ice Age on the first floor and the more recent fossils on the second floor.
(A) alphabetical
(B) chronological
(C) random
(D) arbitrary

(E) retrospective

440. The new dance troupe£§s gravest problem, one that mars the current production, is a desire for correctness and technical accuracy that ________ both energy and technical accuracy that ________ both energy and musical response.

(A) enhances
(B) stifles
(C) transforms
(D) reflects
(E) supplies

441. The novel Uncle Tom's Cabin, which effectively ________ the unfairness toward black people, was a major influence in ________ the anti-slavery movement.

(A) portrayed...strengthening
(B) attacked...pacifying
(C) glamorized...launching
(D) viewed...appraising
(E) exposed...condemning

442. The number of black hawks has ________ because the encroachments of humans ontheir territory have caused them to ________ their customary breeding places.

(A) multiplied. . . endure
(B) extrapolated. . . alter
(C) increased. . . locate
(D) diminished. . . accept
(E) dwindled. . . shun

443. The observers hope to find out how important ________ foraging is to these endangered shorebirds in order to ________ the importance of restricting nighttime human use of beaches to specific places or times.

(A) nocturnal...ascertain
(B) aerial...convey
(C) underwater...rectify
(D) sporadic...mitigate
(E) desultory...mandate

444. The omniscient narrator stands above the story he is telling, ________ his knowledge of what will occur.

(A) disheartened by
(B) unlimited in
(C) ostracized for
(D) vindicated by
(E) uncertain of

445. The opossum is_____ the venom of snakes in the rattlesnake subfamily and thus views the reptiles not as ________ enemies but as a food source.

(A) vulnerable to. . . natural
(B) conscious of. . . mortal

(C) impervious to. . . lethal
(D) sensitive to. . . deadly
(E) defenseless against. . . potential

446. The patient bore the pain ________ , neither wincing nor whimpering when the incision was made.
(A) histrionically
(B) stoically
(C) sardonically
(D) poorly
(E) marginally

447. The periodic nature of her complaints began to concern us: alarmed by these ________ attacks, we decided to consult a doctor in spite of her opposition.
(A) trivial
(B) recurrent
(C) superficial
(D) spontaneous
(E) tentative

448. The philosopher Auguste Comte ________ the term altruism to ________ unselfish regard for the welfare of others.
(A) avoided...rationalize
(B) coined...denote
(C) applied...lessen
(D) explained...refute
(E) understood...terminate

449. The plot of the motion picture Hoosiers is ________ ; we have all seen this story, the tale of an underdog team going on to win a championship, in one form or another countless times.
(A) inept
(B) absorbing
(C) intricate
(D) controversial
(E) trite

450. The plot of this story is so ________ that I can predict the outcome.
(A) intricate
(B) theoretical
(C) pivotal
(D) trite
(E) fictitious

451. The police feel that the ________ shown by the judges to first offenders unfortunately ________ many youngsters to embark on a life of crime.
(A) understanding...condemns
(B) clemency...encourages
(C) harshness...predisposes

笔 记 区

(D) indifference...directs

(E) intolerance...induces

452. The president was ________ about farm subsidies, nor did he say much about the even more ________ topic of unemployment.

(A) expansive...interesting

(B) wordy...important

(C) uncommunicative...academic

(D) noncommittal...vital

(E) enthusiastic...stimulating

453. The quotation was erroneously ________ to a British poet.

(A) resolved

(B) attributed

(C) activated

(D) relegated

(E) vitiated

454. The reader has the happy impression of watching an extraordinarily inventive and intellectually ________ novelist working at the ________ of her powers.

(A) dishonest...apex

(B) creative...eclipse

(C) fecund...height

(D) effete...limits

(E) amenable...diminution

455. The report was relentlessly ________ to the scientist, interpreting one complex event after another to his ________ .

(A) magnanimous...dismay

(B) disparaging...initiative

(C) innocuous...indifference

(D) hostile...discredit

(E) obsequious...detriment

456. The sea was so rough that the safest thing to do was to seize the railing of the ship and hang on; walking was too ________ a pastime.

(A) leisurely

(B) pleasant

(C) tempting

(D) precarious

(E) prosaic

457. The selection committee for the exhibit was amazed to see such fine work done by a mere ________ .

(A) connoisseur

(B) artist

(C) amateur

(D) entrepreneur

笔 记 区

(E) exhibitionist

458. The sergeant suspected that the private was ________ in order to avoid going on the _____march scheduled for that morning.

(A) malingering. . . arduous

(B) proselytizing. . . interminable

(C) invalidating. . . threatened

(D) exemplary. . . leisurely

(E) disgruntled. . . strenuous

459. The seriousness of the drought could only be understood by those who had seen the________ crops in the fields.

(A) copious

(B) deluged

(C) wilted

(D) bumper

(E) diversified

460. The seventeenth-century writer Mary Astell was a rare phenomenon, a single woman who maintained and even ________ a respectable reputation while earning a living by her pen.

(A) eclipsed

(B) impaired

(C) decimated

(D) avoided

(E) enhanced

461. The stereotypical image of masculinity assumes that weeping is ________ "unmanly"behavior, and not simply a human reaction which may be ________ by either sex.

(A) inexplicably...repented

(B) excessively...discerned

(C) essentially...defined

(D) inherently...adopted

(E) intentionally...exaggerated

462. The surgeons were worried about the possibility of finding ________ growth in the patient.

(A) a benign

(B) a superficial

(C) an organic

(D) an operable

(E) a malignant

463. The systems analyst hesitated to talk to strangers about her highly specialized work, fearing it was too ________ for people uninitiated in the computer field to understand.

(A) intriguing

(B) derivative

(C) frivolous

(D) esoteric

(E) rudimentary

笔 记 区

464. The tapeworm is an example of ________ organism, one that lives within or on another creature, deriving some or all of its nutriment from its host.
(A) a hospitable
(B) an exemplary
(C) a parasitic
(D) an autonomous
(E) a protozoan

465. The teacher suspected cheating as soon as he noticed the pupil's ________ glances at his classmate's paper.
(A) futile (B) sporadic
(C) furtive (D) cold
(E) inconsequential

466. The term mole rat is a ________ , for these small, furless rodents are neither moles nor rats.
(A) pseudonym
(B) digression
(C) misnomer
(D) nonentity
(E) preference

467. The testimony of eyewitnesses is notoriously ________ ; emotion and excitement all too often cause our minds to distort what we see.
(A) judicious
(B) interdependent
(C) credible
(D) unreliable
(E) gratifying

468. The text brims with details, but there are no overarching theses to ________ them.
(A) specify
(B) exaggerate
(C) confound
(D) unify
(E) modify

469. The thought of being trapped in a stalled elevator terrifies me; it brings out all my ________ fears of small, enclosed places.
(A) agoraphobic
(B) kleptomaniac
(C) hypochondriac
(D) therapeutic
(E) claustrophobic

470. The true historian finds the facts about Marlowe and Shakespeare far more interesting than people's unfounded ________ .
(A) complaints
(B) evidence

笔记区

(C) conjectures
(D) qualms
(E) certainty

471. The typist made no effort to be ________ ; she double-spaced the first and third letter, then single-spaced the second, fourth, and fifth letters.
(A) consistent
(B) prompt
(C) amicable
(D) courteous
(E) considerate

472. The villagers fortified the town hall, hoping this improvised ________ could ________them from the guerrilla raids.
(A) stronghold...alienate
(B) refuge...distinguish
(C) bastion...protect
(D) venture...intimidate
(E) disguise...safeguard

473. The younger members of the company resented the domineering and ________ manner of the office manager.
(A) urbane
(B) prudent
(C) convivial
(D) imperious
(E) objective

474. Their married life was not ________ since it was fraught with bitter fighting and arguments.
(A) nubile
(B) tranquil
(C) obvious
(D) cogent
(E) imminent

475. There are too many ________ and not enough serious workers.
(A) sycophants
(B) kleptomaniacs
(C) novices
(D) dilettantes
(E) zealots

476. There is nothing ________ or provisional about Moore's early critical pronouncements; she deals ________ with what were then radical new developments in poetry.
(A) tentative. . . confidently
(B) positive. . . expertly
(C) dogmatic. . . arbitrarily
(D) shallow. . . superficially

笔 记 区

(E) imprecise. . . inconclusively

477. There was some stagecraft behind the supposedly ________ moments photographed by Doisneau; in a legal dispute last year, Doisneau ________ that he had paid two models to pose for his famous The Kiss at the Hotel de Ville.

(A) innocent...disproved

(B) candid...acknowledged

(C) theatrical...regretted

(D) affected...intimated

(E) spontaneous...urged

478. There were ________ in her nature that made her seem an ________ enigma: she was severe and gentle; she was modest and disdainful; she longed for affection and was cold.

(A) aspirations...irreducible

(B) contradictions...inexplicable

(C) distortions...impetuous

(D) disparities...interminable

(E) incongruities...irrelevant

479. These regulations are so ________ that we feel we have lost all our privileges.

(A) stringent

(B) aristocratic

(C) redundant

(D) specious

(E) garish

480. These sporadic raids seem to indicate that the enemy is waging a war of ________ rather than attacking us directly.

(A) retribution

(B) attrition

(C) conquest

(D) subversion

(E) words

481. This latest biography of Malcolm X is a nuanced and sensitive picture of a very complex man, ________ analysis of his personality.

(A) an ineffectual

(B) a telling

(C) a ponderous

(D) a simplistic

(E) an overblown

482. This well-documented book is ________ researched, fluently written, and unfailingly intelligent in tracing the ________ course of its subject's tormented career.

(A) indifferently...triumphant

(B) inadequately...unfortunate

(C) painstakingly...tragic

笔 记 区

(D) carefully...auspicious

(E) thoroughly...promising

483. This well-documented history is of importance because it carefully ________ the ________ accomplishments of Indian artists who are all too little known to the public at large.

(A) recognizes...negligible

(B) overlooks...purported

(C) scrutinizes...illusory

(D) distorts...noteworthy

(E) substantiates...considerable

484. Thomas Jefferson called The Federalist papers "the best commentaries on the principles of government ever written, "and two centuries later they still ________ asthe most ________ statements of American political philosophy.

(A) stand...derivative

(B) rate...abstruse

(C) rank...impressive

(D) fascinate...ambiguous

(E) compete...underrated

485. Those interested in learning more about how genetics applies to trees will have to -________ the excellent technical journals where most of the pertinent material is ________ .

(A) subscribe to. . . ignored

(B) suffer through. . . located

(C) rely on . . . unrepresented

(D) resort to. . . found

(E) see through...published

486. Though Phil had expected to feel overawed when he met Joe Montana, he found the world-famous quarterback friendly and ________ .

(A) querulous

(B) acerbic

(C) domineering

(D) unintimidating

(E) taciturn

487. Though Socrates was ________ by his students who found truth in his teachings, his philosophy constituted ________ to the existent government.

(A) accepted...a benefit

(B) denied...an innovation

(C) appraised...an exception

(D) slighted...a challenge

(E) revered...a threat

488. Though critic John Simon seldom has a good word to say about most contemporary plays, his review of All in the Timing was a total ________ .

(A) mistake

(B) dismissal

笔 记 区

(C) fraud
(D) rave
(E) farce

489. Though financially successful, the theater season, once again, is more noted for its ________ than for its original productions.
(A) musicals
(B) revivals
(C) failures
(D) rehearsals
(E) commercials

490. Though masterminded by the Metropolitan Museum's Guy Bauman, this survey of Flemish paintings in America was clearly a ________ operation, aided by scholars throughout North America.
(A) marginal
(B) derivative
(C) worthwhile
(D) circuitous
(E) collective

491. Though ostensibly teaching posture, Feher brings into play techniques of ballet, yoga, and vocal projection to come up with lessons that can best be described as ________ .
(A) problematic
(B) eclectic
(C) homogeneous
(D) unpretentious
(E) doctrinaire

492. Though set in a mythical South American country, Isabel Allende's novel is ________ the tragic history of Chile.
(A) irrelevant to
(B) rooted in
(C) inconsistent with
(D) exceeded by
(E) indifferent to

493. Though she tried to be happy living with Clara in the city, Heidi ________ for the mountains and for her gruff but loving grandfather.
(A) pined
(B) searched
(C) cheered
(D) labored
(E) trembled

494. Though the ad writers had come up with a highly creative campaign to publicize the company's newest product, the head office rejected it for a more ________ , down-to-earth approach.
(A) innovative

笔记区

(B) drastic
(C) prosaic
(D) noteworthy
(E) philosophic

495. Through her work at the Center for the Family in Transition, Wallerstein has come to see divorce not as a single circumscribed event but as a process that begins during the failing marriage and extends over many years, a ________ of changing family relationships.
(A) continuum
(B) termination
(C) parody
(D) denial
(E) curtailment

496. Throughout his career he demonstrated strong belief in individual faith but powerful ________ about the organized church.
(A) modesty
(B) skepticism
(C) devotion
(D) discernment
(E) ambition

497. To astronomers, the moon has long been an ________, its origin escaping simple solution.
(A) interval
(B) ultimatum
(C) enigma
(D) affront
(E) opportunity

498. To take a ________ attitude, looking down on others as one's inferiors, often is to ________ any chance of favorable relations with them.
(A) promising...negate
(B) patronizing...eliminate
(C) modest...reduce
(D) pertinent...violate
(E) benign...deny

499. Today employers no longer fire or discharge employees; instead, according to the latest ________, they simple "effect a separation. "
(A) digression
(B) overstatement
(C) euphemism
(D) paradox
(E) proverb

500. Tom prided himself on knowing the latest news, the secrets of the rich and the poor; it ________ him that there was something he did not know about his friend.
(A) delighted

笔 记 区

(B) flattered
(C) reminded
(D) galled
(E) reassured

501. Totem craftsmanship reached its ________ in the 19th century, when the introduction of metal tools enabled carvers to execute more sophisticated designs.
(A) roots
(B) conclusion
(C) antithesis
(D) reward
(E) apex

502. Traditional Chinese painters trained by copying their teachers; ________ was reserved for old age, when you might make changes so ________ that they were almost invisible.
(A) imitation...ubiquitous
(B) emulation...dramatic
(C) novelty...marked
(D) originality...slight
(E) honor...petty

503. Trees native to warmer climates are genetically programmed for shorter, milder winters and are therefore ________ to both cold snaps and sudden thaws.
(A) indifferent
(B) restricted
(C) vulnerable
(D) accessible
(E) attributed

504. Trying to prove Hill a liar, Senator Specter repeatedly questioned her ________ .
(A) intelligence
(B) veracity
(C) optimism
(D) autonomy
(E) brevity

505. Uncertain which suitor she ought to marry, the princess ________ , saying now one, now the other.
(A) improvised
(B) vacillated
(C) threatened
(D) compromised
(E) divulged

506. Under the rule of the foreign invaders, the land seemed asleep, save for a small group of rebels who sought to kindle the ________ nationalism of the people.
(A) valid
(B) blatant

笔 记 区

(C) dormant
(D) pretentious
(E) contemplated

507. Unfortunately, excessive care in choosing one's words often results in a loss of ________.
(A) precision
(B) atmosphere
(C) selectivity
(D) spontaneity
(E) credibility

508. Unfortunately, in developing countries rapid economic growth often ________ the overexploitation of natural resources and ________ distribution of wealth.
(A) halts...indiscriminate
(B) holds off...inadequate
(C) leads to...inequitable
(D) continues...evenhanded
(E) goes beyond...ungrateful

509. Unfortunately, the current Broadway season offers some ________ fare that sounds markedly like imitations of previous hits.
(A) epic
(B) radical
(C) formulaic
(D) incongruous
(E) challenging

510. Unlike Sartre, who was born into a cultivated environment, receiving culture in his feeding bottle, so to speak, the child Camus had to fight to ________ a culture that was not ________.
(A) acquire...innate
(B) encourage...barbarous
(C) develop...frivolous
(D) restrain...inferior
(E) justify...conventional

511. Unlike W. E. B. Dubois, who was ________ of the vocational emphasis in black education, Booker T. Washington favored ________ the limited funds available for educating blacks to programs that prepared people for practical jobs.
(A) critical...restricting
(B) aware...confining
(C) suspicious...denying
(D) protective...allotting
(E) appreciative...allocating

512. Unlike her sister, the Widow Douglass, who ________ Huck's minor offenses, Miss Watson did nothing but scold the boy.
(A) believed
(B) rebuked

笔 记 区

(C) condoned
(D) evaded
(E) corroborated

513. Unlike the highly ________ Romantic poets of the previous century, Arnold and his fellow Victorian poets were ________ and interested in moralizing.
(A) rhapsodic. . . lyrical
(B) frenetic. . . distraught
(C) emotional. . . didactic
(D) sensitive...strange
(E) dramatic. . . warped

514. Untempered by any ________ , she spread an ever more militant message to her followers.
(A) conviction
(B) enthusiasm
(C) radicalism
(D) hardship
(E) moderation

515. Upon realizing that his position was ________ , the general ________ his men to retreat to a neighboring hill.
(A) valuable . . . admonished
(B) untenable. . . ordered
(C) overrated. . . forbade
(D) exposed. . . urged
(E) salubrious. . . commanded

516. Using novel concepts and techniques previously unknown in commercial advertising, the ________ advertising campaign broke new ground in the field of marketing.
(A) questionable
(B) interminable
(C) imitative
(D) inadequate
(E) innovative

517. Waiting impatiently in line to see Santa Claus, even the best-behaved children grow ________ and start to fidget.
(A) restive
(B) noisome
(C) sonorous
(D) pungent
(E) ambivalent

518. Was he so thin-skinned, then, to ________ any small ________ at his expense?
(A) support...purchase
(B) repeat...compliment
(C) comprehend...mystery
(D) resent...jest

(E) disregard...insult

519. Watching the hang gliders soar above the fields, I marveled at how they seemed to ________ gravity, hovering in the sky like rainbow-colored birds.
(A) release
(B) adorn
(C) defy
(D) emulate
(E) abet

520. Waving broadly at the still-applauding crowd, the speaker was highly ________ by the ________ response to her talk.
(A) exasperated...vehement
(B) gratified...enthusiastic
(C) bewildered...profound
(D) intimidated...sincere
(E) delighted...skeptical

521. We cannot pardon such ________ act of violence.
(A) an expedient
(B) an egregious
(C) a munificent
(D) a circumspect
(E) an insipid

522. We find it difficult to translate a foreign text literally because we cannot capture the ________ of the original passage exactly.
(A) novelty
(B) succinctness
(C) connotations
(D) ambivalence
(E) alienation

523. We had not realized how much people ________ the library's old borrowing policy until we received complaints once it had been ________.
(A) enjoyed. . . continued
(B) disliked. . . administered
(C) respected. . . imitated
(D) ignored. . . lauded
(E) appreciated. . . superseded

524. We look with pride at our new bridges and dams, for they are works of art as well as of ________.
(A) leisure
(B) aesthetics
(C) drudgery
(D) utility
(E) anachronism

笔 记 区

525. We must overcome his ________ social change if we wish to win his support for this innovative program of home health care for the elderly.

(A) tendency to
(B) endorsement of
(C) antipathy to
(D) respect for
(E) achievement of

526. We need both ornament and implement in our society; we need the artist and the ________ .

(A) beautician
(B) writer
(C) politician
(D) artisan
(E) model

527. We need more men and women of culture and enlightenment in our society; we have too many ________ among us.

(A) pedants
(B) philistines
(C) ascetics
(D) paragons
(E) apologists

528. We were amazed that a man who had been heretofore the most ________ of public speakers could, in a single speech, electrify an audience and bring them cheering to their feet.

(A) enthralling
(B) accomplished
(C) pedestrian
(D) auspicious
(E) masterful

529. Wemmick, the soul of kindness in private, is obliged in ________ to be uncompassionate and even ________ on behalf of his employer, the harsh lawyer Jaggers.

(A) conclusion. . . careless
(B) principle. . . contradictory
(C) theory. . . esoteric
(D) court. . . judicious
(E) public. . . ruthless

530. What made Ann such a fine counselor was her ________ , her ability to put herself in her client's place and feel his emotions as if they were her own.

(A) integrity
(B) empathy
(C) tenacity
(D) impartiality
(E) aloofness

531. What most ________ the magazine's critics is the manner in which its editorial opinions are expressed—too often as if only an idiot could see things any other way.

笔 记 区

(A) belies
(B) impedes
(C) riles
(D) placates
(E) identifies

532. When Doctor Diamond's lab discovered that male and female sex hormones affect the outer layers of the brain in different ways, she was originally ________ to ________ the data because of possible misinterpretations.
(A) hesitant...release
(B) proud...distort
(C) reluctant...assimilate
(D) inclined forge
(E) pleased...locate

533. When Dorothy and her friends realized that, despite his claims, the Wizard of Oz didn't know how to get them back to Kansas, they were sure they'd been______ by a ______
(A) befriended...philanthropist
(B) succored...magician
(C) captured...genius
(D) duped...charlatan
(E) delayed...miser

534. When I listened to her cogent arguments, all my ________ were ________ and I was forced to agree with her point of view.
(A) senses...stimulated
(B) opinions...confirmed
(C) preconceptions...substantiated
(D) questions...interpolated
(E) doubts...dispelled

535. When clay dries out, it loses its plasticity and becomes less ________.
(A) synthetic
(B) expensive
(C) malleable
(D) tangible
(E) brittle

536. When railroads first began to supplant rivers and canals as highways of commerce, they were regarded as blessings and their promoters were looked upon as ________.
(A) hucksters
(B) upstarts
(C) atheists
(D) benefactors
(E) diehards

537. When such ________ remarks are circulated, we can only blame and despise those who produce them.

笔 记 区

(A) adulatory
(B) chance
(C) rhetorical
(D) redundant
(E) reprehensible

538. When the news of his ________ the enemy became known, he was hanged in effigy.
(A) contempt for
(B) enmity toward
(C) collusion with
(D) conspiracy against
(E) interrogation by

539. When trees go dormant in winter, the procedure is anything but ________ : it is an active metabolic process that changes the plant ________ .
(A) sleepy...radically
(B) pleasant...intermittently
(C) dynamic...majestically
(D) overt...openly
(E) organic...thoroughly

540. When we encounter a tentative thought of our own in someone else's writings, any ________ we may have had of its validity is ________ , and what we were hesitant to believe is confirmed as truth.
(A) assurance...unfounded
(B) intimation...imprudent
(C) doubt...dispelled
(D) proof...unjustified
(E) suspicion...reinforced

541. When we saw black smoke billowing from the wing of the plane, we were certain that disaster was ________ .
(A) unlikely
(B) catastrophic
(C) imminent
(D) undeserved
(E) averted

542. When you learn archaeology solely from lectures, you get only ________ sense of the concepts presented, but when you hold a five-thousand-year-old artifact in your hands, you have a chance to involve your senses, not just your intellect.
(A) an invalid
(B) an anachronistic
(C) an abstract
(D) a specious
(E) a tangential

543. Where lesser scholars would have been ________ by the vast collection of unpublished letters,

笔 记 区

rough drafts, and journals left by Henry James, Leon Edel was emboldened by its discovery and began to plan an ambitious series of studies on the life and works of the novelist.

(A) intrigued
(B) encouraged
(C) incensed
(D) taxed
(E) daunted

544. Whereas most scholars have tended to regard Monteverdi's opera L'Orfeo as the beginning of a tradition, Mr. Pickett sensibly considers it the ________ of one.

(A) origin
(B) example
(C) presence
(D) culmination
(E) birthright

545. Wherever Lao Li travels, he makes slides of contemporary works of art; his archives ________ every meaningful artistic effort in modern China.

(A) deride
(B) ignore
(C) perpetrate
(D) document
(E) abridge

546. While a great deal of change and modernization has taken place in India since 1947, the basic economic arrangements, values, and family roles have been generally ________ .

(A) overturned
(B) stable
(C) modified
(D) complicated
(E) appropriate

547. While some Southern writers see the past as a heavy burden, others see it as a subject for ________ reflection.

(A) gloomy
(B) wearisome
(C) interminable
(D) nostalgic
(E) bleak

548. While the 1940s are most noted for the development of black modern dance, they are also ________ because they were the last gasp for tap dancing.

(A) irrelevant
(B) unfounded
(C) significant
(D) speculative
(E) contemporary

笔 记 区

549. While the movie Spellbound is a testimonial to the powers of psychoanalysis to overcome the evils of unreason, its portrait of the analytic profession is not entirely ________ .

(A) malignant

(B) obscure

(C) adulatory

(D) vehement

(E) derivative

550. Why bother with facts? Facts that are significant we probably already know, and facts that are new seem essentially ________ .

(A) momentous

(B) antiquated

(C) improbable

(D) undemonstrable

(E) trivial

551. Why do some plant stems develop a protective bark that enables them to survive the winter, while others ________ at the first frost?

(A) blossom

(B) adapt

(C) shrivel

(D) mature

(E) wake

552. Why is it that even the most ________ of students occasionally ________ a seemingly simple question, and finds herself unable to determine the correct answer?

(A) conscientious. . . balks at

(B) dogged. . . proposes

(C) intuitive. . . resolves

(D) erudite. . . overlooks

(E) incompetent. . . stumbles over

553. Wincing at the ________ of the interviewer's wording, the scholar was as ________ to words and phrases as a sectarian is to creeds.

(A) brusqueness...indifferent

(B) vagueness...sensitive

(C) repetitiveness...dogmatic

(D) clarity...addicted

(E) fluency...responsive

554. With the evolution of wings, insects were able to ________ to the far ecological comers, across deserts and bodies of water, to reach new food sources and inhabit a wider variety of promising environmental niches.

(A) relate

(B) disperse

(C) transgress

(D) revert

(E) ascend

笔 记 区

555. With the rift between the two sides apparently widening, analysts said they considered the likelihood of a merger between the two corporations to be ________ .

(A) deteriorating

(B) substantial

(C) coincidental

(D) legitimate

(E) plausible

556. You should ________ this paragraph in order to make your essay more ________ .

(A) delete. . . succinct

(B) enlarge. . . redundant

(C) remove. . . discursive

(D) revise. . . abstruse

(E) excise. . . legible

557. Your ________ remarks spoil the effect of your speech; try not to stray from your subject.

(A) innocuous

(B) digressive

(C) derogatory

(D) persistent

(E) enigmatic

笔 记 区

GRE 补充填空题答案

1-20	DDCBB	EACBA	CECDC	EECDD
21-40	CCCCB	DEDDE	DDCDB	BEDCE
41-60	CDCCE	AABEB	CBBAB	DEEBB
61-80	ECBBB	ACCCA	BBEDD	BDCAC
81-100	EEDAB	CDBCC	CAEBC	DEDAC
101-120	AACDC	BBEAB	DDACD	CECDC
121-140	CBBBB	CEADB	DCCED	CCBEC
141-160	CCCDC	BDBCE	ACCDC	EBEAB
161-180	ABDDB	BCBCD	CCCBC	DCACB
181-200	CDEBD	ABDCC	BACDB	EDECB
201-220	CCEAA	DDBEC	BCDAD	ECDDA
221-240	DDCED	EDACC	ADBBC	DBACB
241-260	CBDEA	CDCCD	CCBEB	CCEEC
261-280	DBCBC	BBBDE	AEBAB	CEABC
281-300	EBBBA	BECEB	AAADA	BDADB
301-320	BBCAC	CBCCB	CABEA	EAABB
321-340	EECCD	CCEDD	DCDCA	EDCEB
341-360	CEDBC	ECEDB	BCBCA	ABACA
361-380	BDCCC	ECADA	BEACB	ADCBC
381-400	DCCBD	CDADD	DCDBB	CBDBE
401-420	CCCEB	DBCDD	BCECB	BCDDB
421-440	DDDEA	ADEBC	AEADB	DCCBB
441-460	AEABC	BBBED	BDBCD	DCACE
461-480	DEDCC	CDDEC	ACDBD	ABBAB
481-500	BCECD	DEDBE	BBACA	BCBCD
501-520	EDCBB	CDCCA	ACCEB	EADCB
521-540	BCEDC	DBCEB	CADEC	DECAC
541-557	CCEDD	BDCCE	CABBA	AB

笔记区

图书在版编目（CIP）数据

GRE 填空教程/《GRE 填空教程》编写组编.
—北京：中国环境科学出版社，2002.7
ISBN 7-80163-336-9

Ⅰ.G... Ⅱ.G... Ⅲ.英语-研究生-入学考试-美国-自学参考资料 Ⅳ.H310.41

中国版本图书馆 CIP 数据核字（2002）第 046973 号

出　版　中国环境科学出版社出版发行
（100036　北京海淀区普惠南里 14 号）
网　　址：http://www.cesp.com.cn
电子信箱：cesp@public.east.cn.net
印　刷　北京泰山兴业印务有限责任公司印刷
经　销　各地新华书店经售
版　次　2005 年 1 月第 4 版　2005 年 1 月第 1 次印刷
开　本　787×1092　1/16
印　张　16

定　价　32.00 元